W9-BZV-423

Theological Anthropology

Sources of Early Christian Thought

A series of new English translations of patristic
texts essential to an understanding of Christian
theology
WILLIAM G. RUSCH, EDITOR

The Christological Controversy
Richard A. Norris, Jr., translator/editor

The Trinitarian Controversy
William G. Rusch, translator/editor

Theological Anthropology
J. Patout Burns, translator/editor

Biblical Interpretation in the Early Church
Karlfried Froehlich, translator/editor

Marriage in the Early Church
David G. Hunter, translator/editor

Theological Anthropology

Translated and Edited by
J. PATOUT BURNS

FORTRESS PRESS
PHILADELPHIA

Copyright © 1981 by Fortress Press

All rights reserved. No part of this publication may be reproduced, stored in
a retrieval system, or transmitted in any form or by any means, electronic,
mechanical, photocopying, recording, or otherwise, without the prior permission
of the copyright owner.

Library of Congress Cataloging in Publication Data

Burns, J. Patout.
   Theological anthropology.

   (Sources of early Christian thought)
   Bibliography: p.
   1. Man (Christian theology)—History of doctrines—
Early church, ca. 30–600. I. Title. II. Series.
BT701.2.B87   233'.09'015 81—43080
ISBN 0–8006–1412–7   AACR2

Printed in the United States of America   1-1412

12   13   14   15   16   17

Contents

Series Foreword

Christianity has always been attentive to historical fact. Its motivation and focus have been, and continue to be, the span of life of one historical individual, Jesus of Nazareth, seen to be a unique historical act of God's self-communication. The New Testament declares that this Jesus placed himself within the context of the history of the people of Israel and perceived himself as the culmination of the revelation of the God of Israel, ushering into history a new chapter. The first followers of this Jesus and their succeeding generations saw themselves as a part of this new history. Far more than a collection of teachings or a timeless philosophy, Christianity has been a movement in, and of, history, acknowledging its historical condition and not attempting to escape it

Responsible scholarship now recognizes that Christianity has always been a more complex phenomenon than some have realized with a variety of worship services, theological languages, and structures of organization. Christianity assumed its variegated forms on the anvil of history. There is a real sense in which history is one of the shapers of Christianity. The view that development has occurred within Christianity during its history has virtually universal acceptance. But not all historical events had an equal influence on the development of Christianity. The historical experience of the first several centuries of Christianity shaped subsequent Christianity in an extremely crucial manner. It was in this initial phase that the critical features of the Christian faith were set; a vocabulary was created, options of belief and practice were accepted or rejected. Christianity's understanding of its God, the person of Christ, its worship life, its communal structure, its understanding of the human condition, all were largely resolved in this early period, known as the time of the church fathers or the patristic church (A.D. 100–700). Because this is the case, both those individuals who bring a faith commitment to Christianity and those interested in it as a major religious and historical phenomenon must have a special regard for what happened to the Christian faith in these pivotal centuries.

The purpose of this series is to allow an English-reading public to gain firsthand insights into these significant times for Christianity by making available in a modern, readable English the fundamental sources which chronicle how Christianity and its theology attained their normative character. Whenever possible entire patristic writings or sections are presented. The varying points of view within the early church are given their opportunity to be heard. An introduction by the translator and editor of each volume describes the context of the documents for the reader.

It is hoped that these several volumes will enable their readers to gain not only a better understanding of the early church but also an appreciation of how Christianity of the twentieth century still reflects the events, thoughts, and social conditions of this earlier history.

It has been pointed out repeatedly that the problem of doctrinal development within the church is basic to ecumenical discussion today. If this view is accepted, along with its corollary that historical study is needed, then an indispensable element of true ecumenical responsibility has to be a more extensive knowledge of patristic literature and thought. It is with that urgent concern, as well as a regard for a knowledge of the history of Christianity, that *Sources of Early Christian Thought* is published.

WILLIAM G. RUSCH

Theological Anthropology

I.

Introduction

Theological anthropology investigates the resources, the limitations, and the destiny of the human person. The authors represented in this anthology share the conviction that humanity's present condition does not correspond to God's ultimate purpose and original intention in its creation. Common to all as well is the assurance that human beings are themselves responsible for this disparity. They also demonstrate that the human capacity for failure was either inevitable or the necessary consequence of the perfection God intended humanity to attain. Finally, all firmly believe that, in Christ, God reverses the consequences of the Fall and moves human beings to a beatitude from which they will not again fall. Although they agree in all of these assumptions and assertions, the authors differ significantly in explaining the initial state and vocation of humanity, in estimating the damage done in the Fall, and in describing the resources for recovery provided in Christ.

This introduction presents an overview of a variety of theological anthropologies which enjoyed fairly broad acceptance in early Christianity. Although nearly all of them are represented in the anthology, the theories are here set out in a pure or ideal form with a coherence and completeness seldom found in any single author or text, even those selected for this volume.

THE GNOSTIC MOVEMENT

By the middle of the second century, a Christian form of

the already widespread Gnostic religious movement had emerged. Although it was ultimately judged deviant and heterodox, the Gnostic interpretation of Christ's work gained long-lasting support and influenced the other Christian anthropologies. The Gnostics (e.g., Valentinus, Basilides) identified the material world and the flesh as the source of humanity's difficulties. The human person was characterized as a spirit whose presence in this alien world resulted when God purified the heavenly realm of the consequences of a sin among angelic beings. The human spirit longs to be liberated from matter and to attain a spiritual existence characterized by knowledge of God. The spirit's natural kinship with the divine grounds this desire and provides the principal resource for its fulfillment. God aids this liberation through Jesus Christ, who reminds human beings of their true destiny and shows them the way of life which will liberate the spirit from a dissipating and enslaving concern with material pursuits and then develop its spiritual potential. Its separation from the flesh in death enables the mature spirit to enter into the heavenly realm. Thus the Gnostic anthropology regards the material condition of humanity as a tragic accident for which human beings do not bear primary responsibility. Existence in this world makes no contribution to the eventual salvation of the human person.

Toward the end of the second century Irenaeus of Lyon (d. ca. A.D. 200) composed the most extensive surviving report and refutation of Gnostic doctrines, his *Detection and Overthrow of the Pretended But False Gnosis*, or more popularly, *Against Heresies*. He rejected both the denigration of the flesh and the absolution of humanity from responsibility for the problems of its actual condition. Human beings were originally created in a bodily condition and will attain the perfection of that condition in the eschatological restoration and renewal of the whole creation in Christ. The imperfection of the present condition indicates neither a failure of divine power over matter nor a lack of divine love for humanity. Divine wisdom actually arranged the creation of humanity in an immature state and its gradual growth into perfect happiness

To be truly good, Irenaeus reasoned, human beings must be free; the love of good has value only when a choice of the contrary evil has been rejected. Instead of giving humanity immortality and beatitude at the outset and risking their loss through free choice, therefore, God devised a strategy to foster a firm commitment to good which would then treasure and preserve full goodness once he had finally bestowed it. First he made human beings immature, capable of learning and development through enjoying the fruits of good choices and suffering the consequences of evil ones. By experiencing the contrast between virtue and sin, human beings can come to appreciate, prefer, and preserve the good; they can build a strong commitment which stabilizes them in the preference of good. God then gives immortality and beatitude to such a mature person, who will not neglect and lose his perfection. Although the sufferings of the present age actually result from sinful choices which should be avoided, God uses them as an educational instrument to move human beings to a full and stable happiness.

Some aspects of Irenaeus' theological anthropology are almost commonplaces in the ancient church, such as the assertion that the possibility of sin is essential to the practice of true virtue. He was singular, however, in claiming that humanity was actually created in an immature condition and has progressed through the experience of good and evil. This aspect of his theory was, of course, directed against the Gnostic evaluation of the present human condition as contrary to the divine will, a situation to be escaped rather than accepted and lived as the way to perfection.

THE ASCETIC MOVEMENT

By the middle of the third century, the two movements which produced the dominant anthropologies of the ancient church had begun to flourish: asceticism and Christian Platonism. Although these two tendencies were sometimes

integrated both in practice and in theory, they actually involved significantly different perspectives on the human situation before God and on the nature of salvation and the
means to attain it.

The beginnings of the ascetic movement can be traced back
to the practice of fasting, almsgiving, continence, and even
virginity within local Christian communities. In the third
century the tendency toward a life of fuller self-denial and a
withdrawal from the temptations of urban and village life
quickened. Chaotic social conditions, the instability of the
imperial government, an increasing burden of taxation, and
the systematic persecution of Christians all contributed to the
retreat. While emphasizing the evils of the social environment, which could be escaped by solitude or life in an iso-
lated Christian fraternity, the movement rested on an opti-
mistic estimate of the resources of human nature itself for
maintaining a commitment to good through obedience to
God's commands. In this sense, the ascetics (e.g., Antony of
Egypt, Martin of Tours) were heirs to the spirituality of the
confessors and martyrs: they trusted that God would reward
their fidelity unto death by raising them from the dead and
granting them unending happiness in a paradise which was
occasionally described in sensual terms.

The differences between the condition of Adam and that
of his offspring are, in the ascetic theory, largely environmental. Adam was placed in pleasant surroundings conducive to
his appreciation of God's goodness and there given a clear
command which he could obey without difficulty. He had
that freedom of choice or self-determination which made him
deserving of reward for fidelity and of punishment for disobedience. God intended that Adam do the good; he allowed the capacity for evil only to make his preference of
good free, virtuous, and worthy of reward. Contemporary
human beings are born with this same capacity to choose between good and evil and are given the opportunity to earn an
eternal reward. Like Adam, the individual person can squan-
der his resources by turning to evil. Sinful choices establish

customs within a person, patterns of response to the entice-ments of evil or addictions to forbidden pleasures which make good choice and action increasingly difficult and improbable. The evil customs of a group in a society can establish a whole culture oriented to sin which then undermines an individual's efforts for good. Thus Adam's sin began a process which has made the environment more conducive to sin than to obedi-ence. Sin is everywhere presented for imitation, and true good is hard to discern and accomplish. Custom, in its in-dividual or social forms, cannot deprive a person of his free-dom of choice between good and evil. Cultural orientations actually gain power over a person only through his free con-sent, which appropriates and internalizes them. As free choices have built evil customs and conceded them power over the person, so his free choices can reverse these patterns and supplant them with good customs which facilitate obedi-ence and virtue.

The Christian life can be described as a struggle to serve God in a hostile environment. The person retains the internal resources of human nature: the light of reason to recognize the good, and the freedom to choose it. Like the obstacles, the aids to using these resources are largely environmental. As sinful acts establish an external and even internal environ-ment that promotes evil, so the collaboration of committed Christians can build a community which helps the individual to choose the good, and his own virtuous actions develop cus-toms which stabilize him in fidelity to God. God's grace also intervenes to change the environment. The patriarchs lived well by the resources of human nature alone and maintained their fidelity to God in the most difficult circumstances. When the assimilation of sinful customs had obscured the true good, God clarified his commands in the Mosaic Law, particularly the Decalogue. Prophets and philosophers con-tinued this work, and Christ finally perfected the law in his own teaching. Similarly, the example of virtuous living set by the saints demonstrates the true capacity of human nature and draws others to imitate them. Christ himself provided the 'supreme exhortation both by the example of his life and death and by his exhibition of the promised rewards in his resurrection. The only other, nonenvironmental form of grace generally recognized in this tradition was the forgiveness of the sins of those who heed the call to conversion.

God makes his grace generally available and holds each individual responsible for responding and using it effectively. He gives special assistance only to those who deserve it. Thus differences in individual situations are earned by good or evil merits.

The freedom of self-determination to good or evil, which is the inalienable divine image implanted in humanity at its creation, stands as the foundation of this anthropology. The exercise of this autonomy for good may be enhanced or encumbered by environmental factors whose actual influence, however, depends upon the individual's own prior consent. Through repeated choices a person will orient himself to either good or evil. In the resurrection God will stabilize the just in good as a reward for fidelity and fix the sinner in the evil he has consistently preferred.

The ascetic movement produced a literature which ranges from pastoral treatises on specific practices and virtues to collections of wise observations by desert monks and the popular biographies of such heroes as Antony of Egypt and Martin of Tours. It is here represented by a section of Pelagius' (fl. early fifth century) hortatory *Letter to Demetrias*.

CHRISTIAN PLATONISM

A second tendency in Christian anthropology, Christian Platonism, in the third and fourth centuries shared some of the assumptions and recommended many of the practices grounding the ascetic perspective just considered. It was specifically different, however, in its attempt to assimilate the resources of non-Christian religious philosophy, especially the current forms of the Platonic tradition. In the second century, Justin Martyr (d. ca. 165) had interpreted Christ as the ordering principle in the universe who manifests himself in the natural light of human moral reasoning as well as in the history of Israel. Origen, the third-century Alexandrian theologian (d. ca. 254), elaborated a Christian understanding of the universe which charted the fall of the human spirit into the flesh and its journey of return to God through Christ. His thought dominated Greek Christianity, particularly in the fourth century, and found adherents on both sides of the major dogmatic controversies. Origen's appropriation and development of the allegorical interpretation used by exegetes of the Homeric writings and the Hebrew scriptures provided a method for the prayer and speculation of Christian mysticism.

Christian Platonism identifies the divine image in humanity not as the autonomy of self-determination but as rationality, the human capacity for knowledge of God. It finds a connaturality between the human spirit and the divine Spirit which manifests itself in a desire for union with God in knowledge and love, an innate and inalienable drive of the human toward the divine.

This desire was implanted in a spirit which was brought into existence from nonbeing through change and therefore always remains subject to change. A certain instability afflicts all created beings; they are always either advancing or retreating in goodness and being. A creature can attain stability and fulfillment only by participating in the unchangeable goodness of uncreated being. Thus the human spirit's natural capacity and desire for union with God provides the basic resource for salvation. The material creation, being irrational and thus incapable of union with God, remains subject to a meaningless repetition of growth and decay which is opposed and inimical to the spirit's development into God. In this understanding of the diversity between the nature and destiny of matter and spirit, the divine purpose in joining them to form humanity becomes puzzling and mysterious. Origen himself seems to have considered it the consequence of a prior sin, though many of his disciples attempted less radical solutions.

Those Christian Platonists who affirmed that God originally created human beings as a union of body and spirit also asserted that God subjected the appetites and desires of the body to the governance of the spirit and ordered them to its fulfillment. In its sin and fall the human spirit turned away from God to itself, lost its dominion over the desires of the flesh, and then fell under the spell of sensual satisfactions. Thus the proper order within the human person was reversed: the dynamism of the spirit became the passion which serves bodily appetites. Although he retains a capacity and desire for God, each human being inherits concupiscence, the independence of bodily appetite and the passion which draws spiritual energy to temporal and temporary satisfactions. The conflict can be fully healed only through the dissolution of the flesh in death and its reconstitution in a spiritualized form. During this life, concupiscence can be aggravated by free consent to bodily desires, which adds the power of custom and deepens the person's servitude. Alternately, the spirit can direct itself to God, subdue fleshly desires by ascetical practices, and thereby begin to recover its proper liberty. In fact, the inheritance of concupiscence permits fleshly desire to seduce the spirit and sensitize it to bodily pleasure and pain before a person reflects upon the true destiny of his nature. Thus the spirit regularly forgets itself and falls under the influence of passion.

The Christian life, according to its Platonic interpretation, begins with the revelation of God in Christ; the divine goodness manifests itself in a sensible form to the spirit immersed in matter. Christ arouses the desire for God and teaches the way of life through which the spirit can reestablish its governance over the flesh and pursue its proper finality. The gradual purification of the spirit liberates its desire and clarifies the divine image imprinted in that natural dynamism. The Christian whose heart becomes pure notices the revelation of God in the creation, contemplates his manifestation in the earthly works of Christ, and, through the deeper figurative understanding of the scriptural record of the economy of salvation, moves to an ever-fuller awareness and appreciation of God's goodness.

The human spirit does not attain stability and beatitude by being fixed in a good state it has maintained until death; rather, the constant change to which it is subject as a creature is focused into a steady growth into union with God. God is inexhaustible, and the human desire for God is insatiable. Once the human spirit is freed from the distractions of the flesh and centered on God, the development process accelerates. The more a person knows and loves God, the more he hungers for God. As the desire grows, a relapse into sensual pursuits becomes increasingly improbable. The created spirit can never stop changing; hence its beatitude consists in an unceasing and ever-increasing development in the knowledge and love which unites it to the divine Spirit. This union with God may begin during earthly life, and its joys may be anticipated in mystical prayer.

Platonic Christianity differs significantly from the anthropology of the ascetic tradition. It describes the Christian life as the growth of a spiritual desire for God rather than as the faithful obedience to the divine commands through which one earns a reward in the next life. It conceives of grace as God's operation which revives and nourishes, which removes the obstacles to the development of the desire God created in humanity. The primary grace is God's self-revelation in the economy of creation and salvation which culminates in the incarnation of the Word. Participation in the death and resurrection of Christ, either in baptism or through physical death and resurrection, heals the concupiscence of the flesh and gives it a new, spiritual life. The commandments of God, along with the teaching and example of Christ and his saints, inspire and guide the Christian's purification and development.

Autonomy and self-determination have a more limited significance in this anthropology than in that of the ascetical tradition, because the liberation and development of the spiritual desire displace the earning of a reward as the basic way to salvation. The power of passion can reduce the liberty of the human spirit. The beginning Christian must oppose the force of concupiscence which has afflicted him from birth and for whose power in him he bears a limited personal responsibility. The more adept have not established virtuous customs by which they commit themselves to good; they have liberated and given free rein to a dynamism which God himself planted and nourished in them. Despite this divine initiative, however, free choice retains its significance in the observance of the commandments and in the exercise of asceticism through which the Christian cooperates with the divine action and labors to free the gift of God within him.

This Platonic movement produced an extensive literature in a variety of forms. It ranges from the scriptural commentaries of Origen through the ascetical treatises of Evagrius of Pontus to the sermons of Ambrose of Milan and the early philosophical treatises of Augustine. It is here represented by a sermon of Gregory of Nyssa (d. ca. 395) on the purity of heart which prepares a person to see God.

FOURTH-CENTURY DEVELOPMENTS

The social factors which encouraged the emergence and development of these two traditions within the Christian movement during the second and third centuries were intensified in the fourth. The century began with a violent and sustained persecution named for its instigator, the Emperor Diocletian (reigned 284–305), in which the imperial government attempted to suppress Christianity. The same century ended with the establishment of the Christian church, the destruction of pagan temples, and the enactment of laws against the traditional Roman religion.

The toleration promised Christianity in A.D. 313, when Emperor Constantine brought Licinius to terms at Milan, developed into a collaboration between church and empire Constantine and his successors actively sought the unification of the church and the solution of divisive doctrinal disputes, often as a means to secure their internal political control and strengthen the defense of the empire. Some Christians reacted to the new situation by withdrawing from secular involvement; others actively took up the challenge of adapting their faith and converting the empire.

The ascetical movement flourished not only in the wilderness of Egypt and Palestine, but also in the West and even in the major cities. Some continued the martyrs' opposition to all compromise with the power of this world. They led simple lives of prayer, manual labor, and asceticism alone or in communities organized to train and sustain them in these exercises. Many Christians of the upper classes were captivated by the lives and practices of these simple monks. Some abandoned their positions and responsibilities, choosing to found or enter monasteries in the Holy Land; others remained in their mansions, dedicating themselves to self-denial and the study of the Scriptures. Teachers and guides such as Jerome (d. 420) and Pelagius developed a following among these aristocrats. Pelagius, for example, was an ascetic of British or Irish origin who came to Rome near the end of the fourth century and became a popular exegete and spiritual director. He composed a commentary on the Epistles of St. Paul and treatises on the virtuous life. Joining the exodus of wealthy Romans after the sack of the city in A.D. 410, he went first to Africa and then to Palestine. There, in 413, he composed his letter of exhortation to Demetrias, the daughter of a wealthy widow who had just refused an advantageous marriage in order to consecrate herself to virginity. Other Roman friends, Melania the Younger and her husband Pinianus, later attempted to mediate his dispute with Augustine (354–430).

The growth of this fairly straightforward ascetical spirituality was more than matched by the assimilation of Neoplatonic philosophy and its elaboration into a specifically Christian anthropology and spiritual theology. The toleration and eventual establishment of the Christian church brought significant numbers of well-educated men into its service as bishops and theologians. Cultured laymen involved themselves in religious discussions. Dogmatic questions such as those of the Trinity and the constitution of Christ were debated not only by reference to Scripture but also with the best instruments of philosophical analysis available. These doctrinal disputes all involved questions of salvation: the human condition and the means of overcoming sin. Origen's earlier formulations were developed and perfected first by Athanasius (d. 373) and then by the Cappadocian theologians. Origen also provided the foundation for the mystical theology developed by Gregory of Nyssa and Evagrius of Pontus (d. 399) to guide Christians beyond the practical wisdom and ascetical practices of the Egyptian monks.

Gregory of Nyssa, whose sermon on the sixth beatitude is included here, was born around A.D. 330 in Cappadocia, modern Turkey. His older brother, Basil, who was both a monastic innovator and among the most influential bishops of his day, pressured Gregory into an episcopal post and involved him in theological controversy. His first love was contemplative retirement, an interest nourished by his sister, Macrina, who is presented as his guide and interlocutor in a number of his ascetical treatises. In his sermons on the beatitudes and other spiritual writings, Gregory employed the figurative interpretation of Scripture which applies the text to the spiritual journey of the individual Christian.

AUGUSTINE

Augustine was familiar with both the ascetic and the Neoplatonic traditions. After following the dualistic materialism of the Manichaeans for nine years, in A.D. 384 he was converted to a Platonic form of Christianity through the instrumentality of Ambrose of Milan (d. 397). Though this new dualism of spirit and flesh remained evident in his writings, his return to his native Africa in 388 and his subsequent entrance into the service of the church at Hippo as presbyter and then bishop brought him under the influence of a popular form of the ascetical tradition which assumed a greater unity between body and soul. His focus shifted from the spirit's release from bodily constraints to the task of moving his congregation to serve God by observing his commandments in order to earn eternal life. The Donatist controversy over the nature of the church provided the impetus for his developing a new and radically different view of humanity's condition before God.

The overwhelming majority of Christian writers had simply assumed that no one could make progress toward or attain salvation apart from union with Christ through the visible communion of his church. Augustine's engagement in the struggle between the Catholic and Donatist communions, which had already dragged on for nearly a century, brought this assertion to a prominent position in his thought. He inferred that all who were not joined to Christ by faith, baptism, and adherence to the Catholic communion must be condemned eternally. Moreover, he reasoned, without the grace provided in Christ, no one can do anything to advance his salvation. Thus Augustine concluded that human nature has no intrinsic and inalienable power to do salvific good and developed his characteristic doctrine of the distinction of nature and grace. Similarly, the affirmation of the inheritance of the guilt of Adam's sin proved necessary to justify the condemnation of infants who were not joined to Christ in baptism.

Augustine had begun to elaborate a radically new anthropology. The natural desire for God which he masterfully described in his *Confessions* had, by the opening of the controversy with Pelagius in A.D. 411, been recognized as a gift of the Spirit of Christ, not an inalienable endowment from the Creator. This grace of charity changed the orientation of the sinful will from self and sensual satisfactions to God, who was now loved for his own sake. Charity also moved a person to the love of neighbor and of the good works which God commands; it fulfilled the basic command of love of God and made all other virtuous action salvific. Attempts to keep the commandments which were motivated not by this love of God but by fear of punishment or hope of reward could be recognized as self-serving and thus contrary to the foundational command to love God above all else. Since everyone outside the church, especially the Donatists who refused Catholic communion, lacked this gift of love of God and neighbor, their apparent obedience to the commandments failed to advance their salvation. They would be condemned for the inherited sin of Adam and for personal sins they had added.

In paradise, Augustine explained, humanity had originally been endowed with the Spirit's gift of charity. The love of God springing from this grace established a freedom of choice between good and evil. In Adam and Eve, neither the environment nor the desires of the flesh placed any obstacles to their love of God and their performance of the good works he commanded. They were governed by the merit-reward economy described by the ascetic anthropology and could easily have earned eternal life. In their rebellion, they and all their children, who were still one with them, lost the gift of charity, were subjected to the revolt of the flesh against the spirit, and incurred the guilt which is transmitted by carnal generation.

In this fallen condition, asserted Augustine, the human person lacks the resources to love and choose the good which he can still recognize through the natural light of reason, the revelation of the commandments, the teaching and example of Christ. In the absence of the grace of charity, he is morally and religiously impotent, incapable of moving toward salvation. Although he may struggle against the power of concupiscence and restrain his fleshly appetites, he only overcomes one passion by another or by the fear of punishment rooted in self-love. Without the grace of Christ, a person's freedom of choice is in servitude to sin, selfishly choosing among evils.

The preaching of the gospel and the gift of faith move such a sinner to abandon his own resources and to pray for the grace by which he might love and perform good. The Spirit's gift of charity establishes a true freedom of choice by bestowing the capacity and inclination to love and prefer the good.

The love of God opposes the power of concupiscence, strengthening a person to maintain and act upon his commitment to good. As God increases his gift of charity, the Christian's freedom gradually grows into a liberty in good, a dynamic tendency in which the probability and occurrence of sin decrease.

The person who perseveres in such good will and action will receive the vision of God and the fullness of divine love. In the resurrection, his flesh is purified and oriented to the spirit's delight in God; his freedom is fully transformed by charity so that he cannot fall back into evil. Human freedom, Augustine specified, can be found in three conditions: in slavery before grace, in Christian choice under grace, in the full liberty of glory.

Augustine retained significant features of the established anthropologies; but he challenged each of them, particularly in his conception of the capacity of fallen humanity to respond to environmental grace and earn a reward or achieve a stable goodness. He agreed with Platonic Christianity by grounding freedom of choice in a more fundamental desire for Supreme Good. Like the Platonists, Augustine described self-determining choice between good and evil as a middle stage of liberty in goodness. Before God grants a person the love for Himself, that person exercises no option for good; once God brings this love to perfection, the person will not actually choose to turn away. The ascetics accounted for this experience of difficulty or ease in choosing and accomplishing good by reference to the power of evil or good customs rather than the development of a more basic desire. Neither the ascetics nor the Platonists were prepared to admit that human nature could lose the capacity to desire and choose the good as God required; nor would they allow that human nature received it as the fruit of grace rather than possessing it as the inalienable property of nature.

Augustine's doctrine of the efficacy and gratuity of the divine gift also differed from that of the established anthropologies. While retaining the ascetic notion of reward, he explained that a divine operation rather than an independent human achievement actually fulfills the qualifying conditions. When the meritorious good action is the work of grace, the reward itself becomes gratuitous. In particular. he asserted that the transitions from sin to grace and from grace to glory are accomplished by a divine operation which itself causes and sustains the appropriate human cooperation. An interior gift of faith accompanies the exterior preaching of the gospel and effectively moves the chosen person to repent and to pray for the further gift of charity. Without such efficacious grace, Augustine argued, the preaching of the gospel does not provoke faith in the sinner. Similarly, a Christian attains eternal glory only if a divine operation maintains him in good willing and performance until the end of his life. Without such effective assistance, the Christian's commitment to good would eventually succumb to the drag of concupiscence and the temptations of the evil world.

In opposition to the Platonic anthropology, Augustine affirmed that the beginning, the increase, and the fulfillment of charity are all gifts of God's own love rather than the gradual development of an innate human desire through asceticism and contemplation. In the crucial transitions from sin to goodness to glory, he denied the human person a capacity for autonomous response and cooperation with the initiative of God's grace. He conceded that God gave the angels and the first human beings the opportunity to earn a reward by independent cooperation with the gift of charity. In view of the failures within this original economy, however, God himself ensures the success and salvation of his elect.

This doctrine of the gratuity and efficacy of grace challenges the Platonist and ascetic assumption that a person's independence in cooperating with grace is integral to human dignity and divine justice. The Augustinian system gives God exclusive credit for beginning and completing the process of salvation. He charges human beings with responsibility for the loss of charity in Adam, even though he asserts that this goodness can be regained and maintained only by the graces of conversion and perseverance, which can be neither earned nor preserved through the resources of fallen human nature.

Augustine was prepared to recognize the various forms of divine assistance which were proposed by the other anthropologies: the divine commands inherent in reason and clarified in the law, the teaching and the example of Christ, the promise of reward and threat of punishment. Yet he insisted that these external forms of help were radically inadequate. They can only supplement the interior graces of conversion, charity, and perseverance which change a person's dispositions, draw him to God, and then maintain him in the love and performance of good. Augustine's denial of an inalienable human capacity for good and his assertion of the efficacy of divine operation in the saved sparked a long and often bitter controversy over the relation of nature and grace.

The controversy with Pelagius, during which Augustine enunciated his new anthropology, began with the trial for heresy of Pelagius' disciple, Caelestius, in Carthage in A.D. 411. A prominent layman asked Augustine's opinion on the condemned teaching that human nature had the capacity to avoid all sin and that infants were born in the original state of Adam. Augustine replied to these questions and subsequently to others raised by Pelagius' treatise, *On Nature*. In 415, Pelagius successfully defended himself against two challenges by Spaniards living in Palestine and began to proclaim the vindication of his doctrine. African synods condemned his teaching twice in the summer of 416 and secured the concurrence of Innocent, the bishop of Rome, in their decisions. His successor, Zozimus, received appeals from Caelestius and Pelagius the following year. He failed to perceive any error in their statements of faith and instructed the African bishops to consider the matter more carefully. In a council at Carthage in May 418, the bishops issued a new and fuller condemnation of Pelagian errors. They affirmed Augustine's teaching on inherited guilt and asserted the necessity of the divine gift of charity for any good choice or action. At the same time, the Western emperor, Honorius, acted upon the earlier condemnations and exiled Pelagius and Caelestius. Zozimus concurred in these decisions.

While Augustine was still in Carthage for the council of 418, he received a letter from the Roman aristocrats Melania and Pinianus, whose acquaintance he had already made in Hippo. They reported a meeting with Pelagius in Palestine and their complete satisfaction with his doctrine and sincerity. They suggested that Augustine cease his campaign and come to terms with him. Augustine quickly replied with twin treatises, *On the Grace of Christ* and *On Original Sin*, in which he exposed the intentional ambiguity of Pelagius' statements and explained the foundations of his own doctrine. The first of these is contained in this volume.

During this period Augustine addressed letters to many influential Christians in Italy to gain their support against Pelagius' teaching. The letter sent to the Roman presbyter Sixtus in the fall of 418 is actually a treatise on the efficacy and gratuity of the initial grace of conversion. Seven years later, monks in an African monastery at Hadrumetum read a copy of this letter and were troubled by Augustine's apparent denial of a person's freedom to dissent, to refuse the grace of God which moves him to convert and to persevere in good. If God causes the sinner to convert and accept his grace, they reasoned, no one should correct or exhort another; rather one should pray to God to change and preserve the other. Augustine clarified and defended his position in *On Grace and Free Choice* in 425 and *On Rebuke and Grace* in 426. These treatises provoked a further reaction from ascetics in southern Gaul. These objectors acknowledged the divine initiative in calling sinners to conversion without regard for any prior merits of an individual, but they denied Augustine's affirmation that God does not await an independent human acceptance and cooperation with his grace. In particular, they rejected his doctrine of perseverance in good by means of a grace which its recipient could not lose by negligence or sin. Augustine responded to these objections, and a debate had begun which would continue for centuries. This second stage in the controversy is represented here by a selection from *On Rebuke and Grace*.

THE AUGUSTINIAN TRADITION

A century later, in A.D. 529, Caesarius of Arles (d. 542) used the gathering of bishops and prominent laymen at the dedication of a new church in Orange as an opportunity to strike a blow against the opponents of Augustine's doctrine of grace. This synod asserted the distinction of nature and grace which made charity necessary even in humanity's original condition. The inheritance of guilt and the moral impotence of Adam's offspring were also reaffirmed. The gratuity and efficacy of the divine grace which moves a person to repent, to believe in Christ, and to pray for and receive the Spirit's gift of charity were set forth. The canons of this synod, its declaration of faith, their confirmation by the Roman bishop Boniface, and an appended dossier of supporting patristic authorities (which Caesarius gathered largely from Augustine's own citations of his contemporaries) all pass over in silence the efficacious grace of perseverance and the question of predestination. The documents of this synod conclude the anthology.

Augustine's anthropology attained only a limited acceptance even in the Latin church. Yet in securing the rejection of certain central features of the ascetic theory, while retaining many elements of Christian Platonism, he moved Latin Christians toward a theological anthropology not unlike that which gained primacy among the Greeks.

The ascetic assumption that human nature retains its original integrity so that the individual was personally responsible for the actual influence of carnal passion or concupiscence in his choices was not, on the whole, maintained. Christians generally recognized Adam's sin as affecting human nature itself, not just its environment. The fundamental human capacity for good is initially either buried under fleshly appetites or completely lost. The person can or will make no advance toward salvation until a divine initiative grants or awakens his desire for true good.

Although Augustine retained the merit-reward structure of the ascetic understanding of the economy of salvation, he undermined its significance in two ways. He asserted that grace is given without prior merits and that it works its own acceptance and produces good works. Thus merit is itself the fruit of unearned grace. Second, by shifting from performance to intention in evaluating good willing and works, he put into new focus the relation between God and the creature. With Augustine, the union with God in knowledge and love which is fundamental to Platonic Christianity supplanted the obedience offered to a Lord who, in the ascetical view, would reward faithful service.

The shift from a union with God based on command and obedience to a unification in knowledge and love involved a change in the understanding of freedom. For Augustine, autonomous self-determination in good or evil yielded primacy to a liberty of love which draws or carries a person toward the object of his desire. Choice between good and evil is thereby relegated to the initial condition of humanity in Adam or reduced to a transitional stage in which a person who is still attached to evil begins to respond to the attractions of good. As liberty matures, this person ceases to deliberate and decide; he gives himself ever more fully and spontaneously to the increasingly manifest and attractive goodness of God.

The ascetic anthropology never fully disappeared in either East or West. Its central assertions of personal responsibility for choice between good and evil, of the self-denial necessary to overcome evil and establish good customs, of a divine justice which rewards obedience and punishes evil were all appropriate to Christian living in the period between initial conversion and final glorification. Thus it served as a counterbalance to the Platonic and Augustinian traditions in preaching, theology, and religious practice.

The most troublesome thing Augustine uncovered proved to be the gratuity and efficacy of divine grace, that is, the principle that an unmerited divine operation would actually produce the human cooperation appropriate for its salvific effect. The West found this theory somewhat useful in understanding the process of conversion, perhaps because it followed from a realization of the moral impotence of fallen or sinful humanity. Augustine's application of this theorem to perseverance in grace and good works, however, involved the assertion of predestination to glory without prior merits, which was widely rejected even in his own day. Many theologians judged that a gratuitous election of some to glory achieved by an operative grace entailed an equally unearned predestination of all others to condemnation accomplished by withholding the same grace. Those who asserted both were condemned, and the majority were content to avoid the question or reduce predestination to foreknowledge of a person's response to grace.

The authority of Augustine and the religious values involved in the development of his anthropology kept his positions alive even in the face of sustained opposition. A thousand years after his death, European Christians found themselves debating the issues he had raised and unable either fully to accept or totally to reject his formulation of the relation between divine grace and human freedom. The documents of this anthology attempt to set Augustine in context so that he may be recognized as an innovator who fused the Platonic Christianity which had freed him from Manichaeism with the ascetical tradition of North Africa which sustained him and his congregation.

These translations have been made from the best editions available; they are listed in the first section of the Bibliography. The Greek version of the Old Testament and Latin version of the whole Bible which were used by the Fathers sometimes differ significantly from modern critical editions of the scriptural text. The commentary or argument being developed by the patristic author occasionally depends upon the particular version available to him. Hence the translation follows the version which appears in the patristic text and does not conform exactly to any of the modern translations of the Bible.

II.

Irenaeus of Lyon

Book IV   **Chapter 38**

(1) Someone might say, "Why is this? Was God unable to make humanity perfect from the start?" He should realize that because God was not born and always remains the same, he can do anything, as far as depends on himself. The things he made had to be lesser than himself, however, precisely because they were to be made and have a beginning. What was only recently created could not be uncreated; such things fall short of perfection by the very fact of not being uncreated. Because they come later, they are immature; as such they are inexperienced and not trained to perfect understanding. A mother, for example, can provide perfect food for a child, but at that point he cannot digest food which is suitable for someone older. Similarly, God himself certainly could have provided humanity with perfection from the beginning. Humanity, however, was immature and unable to lay hold of it. When our Lord came in the last age to gather all things in himself, therefore, he did not come in the way he was able, but in the way we were able to see him. He could have come to us in his indescribable glory; we, however, could not have borne the greatness of his glory. For this reason, the one who was the perfect bread of the Father offered himself to us as milk for children: he came in human form His purpose was to feed us at the breast of his flesh, by nursing us to make us accustomed to eat and drink the Word of

God, so that we would be able to hold in ourselves the one who is the bread of immortality, the Spirit of the Father.

(2) Thus Paul says to the Corinthians, "I gave you milk to drink, not solid food, because you could not yet receive solid food" [1 Cor. 3:2]. He means: I taught you about the coming of the Lord in a human way; because of your weakness, the Spirit of the Father has not yet rested upon you. "For when envy, strife and factions exist among you," he says, "are you not being carnal and walking in human ways?" [1 Cor. 3:3]. This means that they did not yet have the Spirit of the Father because of their imperfection and the inconstancy of their conduct. Still, the Apostle could have given them solid food. Anyone upon whom the apostles imposed hands received the Holy Spirit, who is the food of life. They could not hold him, however, because their capacity for dealing with God was still weak and undeveloped. Similarly, God could have given humanity perfection in the beginning. Humanity, however, had just been made; it could not receive it, or hold it once received, or preserve it once held. The Word of God, then, did not take on humanity's immaturity for his own sake, since he was perfect; rather, because of humanity's immaturity was he made susceptible of being grasped by humans. The inadequacy and impossibility were not on God's part but on the part of humanity, since it was not uncreated but had just been made.

(3) God's power, wisdom, and goodness are all demonstrated at once: power and goodness in his freely creating and establishing things which do not yet exist; wisdom in his making things which follow in order, which go together, which are well arranged. Through his immense goodness, some of them develop, continue for a long time, and reach the glory of the uncreated. God generously bestows on them what is good. Though as created, they are not uncreated; still since they continue for long ages, they will take on the strength of the uncreated. God will give them everlasting endurance.

God therefore has dominion over all things since he alone

is uncreated, is before all things, and is the cause of the existence of all things. All else remains subjected to God. Submission to God is incorruption, and continuance in incorruption is the glory of the uncreated. Through this system, such arrangement, and this kind of governance, humanity was created according to the image and established in the likeness of the uncreated God. The Father decided and commanded; the Son molded and shaped; the Spirit nourished and developed. Humanity slowly progresses, approaches perfection, and draws near to the uncreated God. The perfect is the uncreated, God. It was therefore appropriate for humanity first to be made, being made to grow, having grown to be strengthened, being stronger to multiply, having multiplied to recover from illness, having recovered to be glorified, and once glorified to see its Lord. God is the one who is going to be seen; the vision of God produces incorruptibility; incorruptibility makes a person approach God.

(4) People who do not wait for the period of growth, who attribute the weakness of their nature to God, are completely unreasonable. They understand neither God nor themselves; they are ungrateful and never satisfied. At the outset they refuse to be what they were made: human beings who are subject to passions. They override the law of human nature; they already want to be like God the Creator before they even become human beings. They want to do away with all the differences between the uncreated God and created humans. Thus they are more unreasonable than the dumb animals. The beasts do not blame God for not making them human; rather, by the fact of its creation each gives thanks for being made. We, however, complain that instead of being made gods from the beginning, we are first human and then divine. Yet God followed the simplicity of his goodness in doing this. To prevent anyone from considering him jealous or lacking in generosity, he says, "I said that you are gods, all children of the Most High." To us, however, who could not stand to bear the might of divinity, he said, "You, however, will die like human beings" [Ps. 82:6, 7]. He speaks here of

two things: of the generosity of his gift, then of our weakness and our having dominion over ourselves. In his generosity he freely gave what was good and made human beings like himself in their having control over themselves. In his foresight he knew human weakness and what would result from it. In his love and power he will surpass the substance of our created nature. It was appropriate that the nature first appear and only later that the mortal be surpassed and absorbed by immortality, the corruptible by incorruptibility; that by acquiring the knowledge of good and evil, human beings should be made according to the image and likeness of God.

Chapter 39

(1) Human beings acquired the knowledge of good and evil. Good is to obey God, to believe in him, to keep his command; this means life for human beings. On the other hand, not to obey God is evil; this is death for human beings. God has exercised patience, and human beings have come to know both the good of obedience and the evil of disobedience. Thus by experiencing them both the mind's eye would choose the better things with discernment and never become sluggish or negligent of God's command. By learning through experience the evil of not obeying God, which would deprive them of life, human beings would never try it. Rather, knowing the good of obeying God, which preserves their life, they would diligently maintain it. Human beings have this twofold power of perception which gives the knowledge of good and evil so that they might choose the better things intelligently. How can someone be intelligent about good when he does not know what is contrary to it? Certain understanding of the issue to be decided is more solid than a conjecture based on guessing. The tongue experiences sweet and sour by tasting; the eye distinguishes black from white by seeing; the ear perceives the difference between sounds by hearing. In this same way, by experiencing good and evil, the mind comes to understand good and is strengthened to preserve it by obeying God. First by repentance it rejects dis-

obedience because it is bitter and evil. By grasping the nature of what is opposed to the sweet and good, it will never again try to taste disobedience to God. If a person avoids the two-fold power of perception and the knowledge of both of these, therefore, he implicitly destroys his humanity.

(2) How will one who has not yet become human be God? How can one just created be perfect? How can one who has not obeyed his Maker in a mortal nature be immortal? You should first follow the order of human existence and only then share in God's glory. You do not make God; God makes you. If you are God's artifact, then wait for the hand of the Master which makes everything at the proper time, at the time proper for you who are being created. Offer him a soft and malleable heart; then keep the shape in which the Master molds you. Retain your moisture, so that you do not harden and lose the imprint of his fingers. By preserving your structure you will rise to perfection. God's artistry will conceal what is clay in you. His hand fashioned a foundation in you; he will cover you inside and out with pure gold and silver. He will so adorn you that the King himself will desire your beauty [Ps. 45:11]. If, however, you immediately harden yourself and reject his artistry, if you rebel against God and are ungrateful because he made you human, then you have lost not only his artistry but life itself at the same time. To create belongs to God's goodness; to be created belongs to human nature. If, therefore, you commit to him the submission and trust in him which are yours, then you hold on to his artistry and will be God's perfect work.

(3) If, however, you do not believe in him and you run from his hand, then the cause of your imperfection will be in you who did not obey, not in him who called. He sent messengers to call to the wedding; those who did not obey him deprived themselves of the royal banquet [Matt. 22:1–14].

God's skill is not deficient; he can raise up children to Abraham from the stones [Matt. 3:9]. The person who does not acquire that artistry is himself the cause of his imperfection. People who have blinded themselves do not thereby make the light itself inadequate. The light remains just as it is while those blinded through their own fault are plunged into darkness. As the light does not subdue anyone by compulsion, neither does God force the person who refuses to retain his artistry. Those who stood outside the paternal light and transgressed the law of liberty had been given free choice and power over themselves; they separated themselves through their own fault.

(4) God, of course, foreknew all this and arranged appropriate dwelling places for both kinds of people. On those who seek and return to the light of incorruptibility, he graciously bestows the light they desire. For those who despise it and turn away, who run from it and blind themselves, he has prepared the darkness fitting for opponents of the light. Those who fled from submission to him he has subjected to an appropriate punishment. Submission to God is eternal rest. Thus those who flee the light have a setting befitting their flight; those who flee eternal rest have a dwelling appropriate to their flight.

Since, however, God is surrounded by everything that is good, those who decide to run from God deprive themselves of all good things. Then, deprived of all the good things associated with God, they will fall into his just judgment. Those who have fled the light justly dwell in darkness; those who flee rest will justly abide in punishment. In the case of this temporal light, those who abandon it subject themselves to darkness. They are themselves the cause of their desertion by the light and dwelling in darkness. The light itself does not cause their situation, as we have already said. In the same way, those who run from God's eternal light, which contains all good things in itself, are themselves the cause of their dwelling in eternal darkness, of their being destitute of everything good. They made themselves the cause of their dwelling in such a place.

III.

Gregory of Nyssa

SERMON ON THE SIXTH BEATITUDE

Imagine how it must feel to peer out over the open sea from a high mountain ridge. That is what my mind feels when it peers down from the loftiness of the Lord's saying, as from a mountain peak, upon the infinite depth of thought to which it gives vantage. One frequently comes across this scene in maritime districts: a mountain is, as it were, split in half. The sea has worn away the side that faces it in a straight line from the summit to the foot. But from the upper lip of this sheer cliff there juts forward a rocky projection, which tilts out over the sea. What must a person feel when he peers down at the sea beneath him from such a vantage point? As in his case, vertigo seizes me as I find myself suspended over the awesome implications of our Lord's saying "Blessed are the pure in heart, for they shall see God" [Matt. 5:8]. God offers himself as a spectacle for those whose hearts are purified!

But, says the great Apostle John, "No one has ever seen God" [John 1:18]. And the sublime Apostle Paul seconds him saying, "Whom no one has seen or can see" [1 Tim. 6:16]. This is the smooth, sheer rock whose surface discloses not a single foothold for our comprehension, the rock which Moses pronounced inaccessible in his laws. For he strips away the possibility that our understanding could approach it by asserting, "For no one can see God and live" [Exod. 33:20]. But, you object, "To see God is eternal life." John, Paul,

This selection was translated by Joseph W. Trigg.

and Moses, the pillars of the faith, nonetheless unanimously pronounce it unattainable.

Now do you see why my soul grows dizzy at the contemplation of the profundity of the matters embraced in this saying? If God is life, he who does not see him fails to see life. But the prophets and apostles, closer to God than we can hope to be, solemnly declare that no one can see God. Is our hope reduced to nothing?

No, it is not. The Lord himself sustains our faltering hope, just as he sustained Peter. When Peter was in danger of drowning, he made him stand once more on the firm and solid surface of the water. If, then, the hand of the Logos should reach out to us, even as we are struggling in the uncertainties which the profundity of these ideas entails, and establish us firmly in a different interpretation, we should cease to be fearful, as the Logos has grasped us and he leads us firmly by the hand. For "Blessed," he says, "are the pure in heart, for they shall see God" [Matt. 5:8].

This promise is so great that it exceeds the utmost imaginable degree of blessedness. Could anyone, once he has received it, desire anything more? Would he not already possess all things in the object of his vision? Remember that "seeing" in scriptural usage means the same thing as "possessing." Cases in point are: "That you might behold the good things of Jerusalem" [Ps. 128:5], instead of, "That you might find them," which is what the phrase actually means; or, "Let the impious person be taken away, that he may not behold the glory of the Lord" [Isa. 26:10], where the prophet's "not behold" means "not participate in." Will not he, then, who sees God possess, in this vision, every possible good thing: everlasting life, eternal imperishability, deathless blessedness, the true light, the sweet and spiritual voice, inaccessible glory, ceaseless exultation, and the ultimate good? The promised blessedness includes all this!

But as we have seen, this vision comes only through purity of heart. Again my mind reels. Is not purity of heart unattainable, a thing beyond the capacity of human nature? It certainly seems so, if this is the way one sees God. After all, Moses and Paul declared that neither they nor anyone else could see God. Must we not conclude that what the Logos himself offers us in this beatitude must be unattainable? What use is it to know how God is to be seen, if the possibility of seeing him does not exist for us? It seems that we are in the same situation as if someone should say that it is blessed to be in heaven, since we could behold there what is not to be beheld in this life. Now if, in saying this, he were to provide some means of getting to heaven, the information that it is most blessed to be in heaven would be very useful to those who heard him. But since there is absolutely no way to ascend to heaven, what good is the knowledge of the blessedness there? It only saddens those who have learned to long for joys which the impossibility of such an ascent makes unattainable.

However, would the Lord really command us to do something that is beyond our nature and issue a commandment whose enormity oversteps our human capacity? That is not possible. He would not order naturally wingless creatures to become birds, or creatures fitted for life on dry land to live under water. If in all other cases his ordinances are adapted to the capacity of those who receive them, and he forces no one beyond nature, we may then conclude by logical inference that the reward which is offered in this beatitude is not beyond hope.

Is it then possible that Paul, John, and Moses, or anyone else of their stature, should have fallen short of the height of this blessedness—Paul, that is, who said, "There is laid up for me a crown of righteousness, which the Lord, the righteous judge, will award to me" [2 Tim. 4:8]; or John, who leaned on Jesus' breast; or Moses, who heard from the voice of God, "I know you beyond all others" [Exod. 33:17]? No one doubts that these men, who proclaimed that the comprehension of God is beyond our ability, were most blessed.

Thus, if blessedness arises from the vision of God, and that in turn from purity of heart, it follows that purity of heart is not impossible.

How can we, then, accept the claims of those, Paul included, who say that the comprehension of God is beyond our capacity? Does not the Lord himself contradict them in his promise that the pure of heart shall see God?

At this point a digression is in order if our discussion is to resume the right course. To begin with, there is no question but that the divine nature, in and of itself, or essentially, is far beyond any attempt we might make to apprehend it. Our conjectures, however apt they may be, cannot so much as approach it. We have no ability whatsoever to comprehend such things, and there has been discovered no discernible approach to what is, after all, impossible to begin with. This is what the great Apostle Paul meant when he called God's ways "untraceable" [Rom. 11:33]. Reason, that is, cannot even approach the way that leads to the knowledge of the divine essence. Nor has anyone ever discovered the slightest perceptible trace of a mode of conjecture that would enable us to know a matter that is beyond knowledge. Since it is the case that God is, by nature, beyond all nature, then he who is invisible and uncircumscribed must be apprehended, if he is to be apprehended at all, by some other means.

Now, as a matter of fact, there are a number of ways in which we can apprehend God. It is possible, through the wisdom perceptible in all things, to perceive aptly him who made all things in wisdom. For just as we can, in a manner of speaking, apprehend the artisan in the finished products that exhibit his skill, so, as we examine the order of creation, we can obtain some notion of the wisdom, if not of the essence, of him who made all things wisely [Ps. 104:24]. Also, if we consider the cause of our own existence, we recognize that we owe it not to necessity but to God's free and beneficent choice; thus we comprehend, if not his essence, then at least his goodness. Similarly, we arrive at the comprehension of God by means of concepts that guide our thoughts beyond the best and highest things in every category, so that each of these lofty concepts brings God into our sight. Concepts such as power, purity, imperturbability, a character uncontaminated by any contrary, and so on, all stamp on our souls the image of his divine and lofty attributes. This digression therefore shows how the Lord's promise that the pure in heart shall see God does not contradict Paul's statement that no one has seen or ever can see God [1 Tim. 6:16]. At the very least, it has been demonstrated that he who is invisible in his nature has become visible in his activities, being seen in the things that surround him.

The view that God can be understood analogically from the comprehension of his activities, however, does not exhaust the meaning of this beatitude. Such comprehension, if we understand it simply as the intellectual apprehension of an underlying wisdom and power arrived at on the basis of the harmony of the universe, is as accessible to the wise of this world as it is to the pure in heart. An example will illustrate why I think that the noble sentiments of the beatitude regarding those who see the object of their longing point to something beyond this. Bodily health is a good thing in human life, but we call someone blessed only if he actually is healthy, not if he simply has a theoretical knowledge of health. After all, if a person were to deliver a discourse in praise of good health and then fall ill from eating tainted or unwholesome food, what would he gain from his speech? The same principle holds in our case. The Lord does not say that it is blessed to know something theoretically about God but to possess God in oneself: "Blessed are the pure in heart," he says, "for they shall see God" [Matt. 5:8].

Now I do not think that this means that God has offered a vision of himself, face to face, to those who have purified the eyes of their souls. But perhaps he explains what the noble sentiments of the beatitude offer us more straightforwardly in another context, namely, when he says, "The kingdom of God is within you" [Luke 17:21]. This verse leads us to the conclusion that they who have cleansed their hearts of all creaturely passions behold the image of the divine nature in their own inner beauty. And it seems to me that the incarnate Logos incorporated the following advice in those brief words. He might say, You human beings, who desire to contemplate what is truly good, do not despair of beholding the object of your desire just because you have heard that the divine majesty is exalted above the heavens, so that his glory is unsearchable, that his beauty is indescribable, and that his nature is incomprehensible. For that which is accessible, the measure of the comprehension of God, is within you. Thus you share essentially in this good thing, in your very nature, with him who made you. For God has stamped the image of the good properties of his own essence in your makeup, as when a sculptor carves in wax the image of a sculpture he intends to cast.

Nevertheless, by sullying over the divine imprint, evil has made useless to you the good now hidden by the shameful deeds that overlay it. Therefore, cleanse yourself of the filth caked over your heart by paying close attention to your conduct, and your godlike beauty will again shine forth. Just as the sun's rays shimmer on a piece of steel once a whetstone has removed the rust from it and it produces a luster, so the true splendor of the inner person, which the Lord calls the heart, reappears when it has rubbed off the unsightly blemish that arises from the mold of evil. Once again it apprehends its similarity to its archetype and is good. For that which is similar to the good is assuredly good itself.

Therefore, he who sees himself sees in himself that which he desires. This is the way a person who is pure in heart becomes blessed; beholding his own purity, he beholds the archetype in the image. One can see the sun without actually looking into the sky by viewing its reflection in a mirror, and see it no less genuinely than those who view its circular form in the sky. In the same way you yourselves, if you strain toward the perception of the light, if you return to the grace already prepared for you in the image, will possess in yourselves the object of your search. For purity is freedom from passion, and divinity is alienation from all evil. If, therefore, these things are in you, God is assuredly in you.

Thus, whenever your mind is uncontaminated by any evil, free from passion and separated from every blemish, it is blessed with sharp sight, so that, being purified, it perceives that which is invisible to those who have not been purified. Once the mist of matter no longer obscures the eyes of the soul, it clearly sees the blessed vision in the pure, clear atmosphere of the soul. And what is that blessed vision but purity, holiness, simplicity, and all such luminous emanations of the divine nature through which God is known?

But we have never really doubted that God is to be seen in this way, and the real issue, in doubt throughout our discussion, still perplexes us. He who is in heaven can obviously commune with the wonders there; but, since it is impossible for us to ascend to heaven, it does us no good to discuss such matters. Similarly, there is no doubt that blessedness arises from the purification of the heart; but it appears to be just as impossible to purify the heart of its blemishes as it is to ascend to heaven. What sort of ladder like Jacob's, what sort of chariot like that which carried the prophet Elijah up to heaven, can we find to lift our hearts to the visions above once we have shaken off this earthly burden?

If anyone were to consider the passionate properties that are a necessary part of the soul, he would consider it difficult, indeed impossible, for the soul to be delivered from the evils closely linked to those properties. Our origin is in passion, through passion we grow, and passion ceases only with our death. Evil has thus permeated even our natural constitution, since we have admitted passion into our nature from the outset, and since we have become settled in this malady through habitual disobedience. As in every species, like begets like and the same natural constitution persists, so that what is born is of the same nature as that which bears it: a human being is born from a human being, passionate human from passionate human, sinner from sinner. Therefore we may say that sinfulness is congenital, that we grow up with it, and that it remains with us throughout our life. At the same time, it is hard for us to accomplish virtue even with great sweat and discipline or with extraordinary zeal and weariness. Thus the Bible often teaches us that the way of the kingdom is narrow and wearisome, while the way that leads to destruction through the performance of evil deeds runs pleasantly and smoothly downhill. Nonetheless, the Bible does not present the virtuous life as utterly impossible, and it provides us the marvelous deeds of some great people as examples.

Now there are two possible meanings for the vision of God promised in the gospel. One of these is the knowledge of the underlying nature of all things; the other is to have communion with God through purity in our life. The first kind of knowledge the saints uniformly consider impossible, but the second the Lord himself promises in the Sermon on the Mount, saying, "Blessed are the pure in heart, for they shall see God" [Matt. 5:8].

How can I become pure, do you say? Well, you can learn almost anywhere in the gospel. Let us run through the precepts of the Sermon on the Mount as an example of its teaching on how to purify the heart. The Bible classifies evil under two heads: the one is the evil committed in actual deeds, the other is the evil that accompanies our thoughts. In the Old Law it punishes manifestly unrighteous deeds. In the New Law it does not simply punish wicked deeds, but also assures that they will not arise to begin with. After all, the surest way to liberate us from evildoing is to remove evil from the human faculty of choice.

Since there are many kinds and forms of evil, in the Sermon on the Mount the Lord has established the appropriate cure for each kind. Since we always seem to have a weakness for it, he begins his discussion with anger, the passion that most frequently dominates us, and ordains that we be meek. "You have been taught," he said, "by the Old Law, 'You shall not kill'; now learn to keep your soul free from all anger against your fellows" [Matt. 5:21–22]. He did not entirely forbid anger, for righteous indignation is still legitimate, but by this precept he utterly quenches unjustifiable anger against one's brother, for he says, "Everyone who is angry with his brother without good cause . . ." [Matt. 5:22]. The addition of "without good cause" shows that anger is at times appropriate, that is, when it boils over for the purpose of chastising sin. This is the sort of anger the Bible previously testified to in the case of Phinehas when, by slaughtering the lawbreakers, he propitiated God's wrath against the people. [Num. 25:6–8].

Having discussed anger, he passes on to the cure for sins that arise from illicit pleasure, and with his precept he removes the unnatural desire for adultery from the heart [Matt. 5:27–28]. Thus, in this sermon you will find the Lord setting straight every variety of sin by means of his legislation. He makes it impossible for unjust violence to occur by refusing to concede the right to self-defense [Matt. 5:38–39]. He banishes the passion of avarice by commanding us to give to him who requisitions our goods even what he is willing to leave us [Matt. 5:40]. He cures our cowardice by commanding us to act disdainfully toward death [Matt. 5:44?]. And, generally speaking, throughout these precepts we find the Lord acting like a plow: he upturns the evil roots of sins in the depths of our hearts, thus enabling us to be cleansed of the thorny fruits those roots sustain. To this end he employs two complementary means for the benefit of our nature: the promise of good things and the teaching that enables us to perform what is required of us. For, if the disinterested zeal for good strikes you as tedious, compare it with the opposite mode of life, and you will find out how much more tedious wickedness is—if not right now, then in the life to come. He who has learned about Gehenna no longer has to be kept from sinful pleasures by toil and zeal; fear alone, having entered his consciousness, will eradicate those passions.

At this point it is appropriate to contemplate an implicit corollary to this teaching, in order to arouse a more fervent desire in us. If the pure in heart are blessed, then those of a diseased mind are miserable, since they shall behold the face of God's enemy. If the divine image itself is stamped on a virtuous life, clearly the vicious life takes on the image and likeness of the devil. Indeed, if God is described under different aspects in various terms for the good—life, light, immortality, and so on—then the converse holds of his enemy, the originator of evil; he may be described as darkness, death, corruption, and whatever is like them.

Therefore, knowing by what means virtue and vice are formed, and since our free choice of the will enables us to choose either of these, let us flee from the image of the devil and put off that wicked mask. Instead, let us reassume the divine image, let us become pure in heart, that we may be blessed, the divine image being formed in us by pure conduct, in Christ Jesus our Lord, to whom be glory for ever and ever. Amen.

IV.

Pelagius

LETTER TO DEMETRIAS

(1) If I were endowed with great intelligence and equal learning, I think I could easily discharge the responsibility of writing this letter. In fact, I cannot escape a great fear of the difficulty of this arduous task. The letter must be addressed to Demetrias, who is not only a virgin of Christ, rich and noble, but who despises her wealth and position in the earnestness of her faith. Whoever admires such singular virtue will find it as difficult to instruct as it is easy to praise. Who would be at a loss for words in which to sing her praises? She was born to the highest social station, reared in great wealth and luxury, ensnared by all the pleasures of this life as though she were bound by the strongest chains. Suddenly she broke free and by her soul's virtue set aside all these bodily goods at once. Like the sword of faith, her will clipped off the flower of the age she was just entering. She crucified her flesh with Christ; she dedicated a holy and living sacrifice to God; for love of virginity she rejected a posterity of the noblest blood. Such a speech would be easy and pleasant; the very richness of the subject would carry it along. We have been asked not to praise this virgin, however, but to instruct her; this task is far more difficult. We must describe the virtues she has yet to attain, not those she has already acquired. We must guide her future course, not praise her past life. The job is all the more difficult because otherwise perfect teaching is barely adequate for a person with such desire to learn and such

eagerness for perfection. She remembers—as well she should—the worldly wealth and reputation she left behind, the pleasures she gave up, the attractions of this life she rejected. Consequently, she is not satisfied with the ordinary way, with a way of life that loses its value in being shared with many companions. She searches for something new and untried; she demands something singular and outstanding. She wants her way of life to be no less extraordinary than her conversion. Noble in the world, she wants to be noble before God. The precious things she gave up as possessions she now seeks in the way she lives. What flood of insight will ever satisfy such a thirst for perfection, the eagerness of so devout a mind? What skill in speaking, what outpouring of mere words could ever describe what this virgin is prepared to accomplish in deeds? We must beg indulgence as we present what gifts we can to adorn the dwelling place of the Lord. Yet we are not afraid that we will further expose ourselves to the attacks of ill will by daring to write to such a noble virgin. Her holy mother has asked us to write. Indeed, with a truly burning desire she sent overseas letters commanding us to do so. The care and diligence with which she originally planted this heavenly seed in her daughter are evident in her solicitude to have others water it. Free of ambition and protected from indiscretion, therefore, we will labor at this project. We are not discouraged, for we trust that our poor ability is aided by the mother's faith and the virgin's merit.

(2) When I have to discuss the principles of right conduct and the leading of a holy life, I usually begin by showing the strength and characteristics of human nature. By explaining what it can accomplish, I encourage the soul of my hearer to the different virtues. To call a person to something he considers impossible does him no good. Hope must serve as guide and companion if we are to set out on the way to virtue; otherwise, despair of success will kill every effort to acquire the impossible. The procedure I have followed in other exhortations should, I believe, be especially observed in this one. Where a more perfect form of life is to be established,

the explanation of nature's goodness should be correspondingly fuller. With a lower estimation of its capacity, a soul will be less diligent and insistent in pursuing virtue. Not realizing what is within, it will assume that it lacks the capacity. A power that is to be exercised must therefore be brought out into full attention, and the good of which nature is capable must be clearly explained. Once something has been shown possible, it ought to be accomplished. The first foundation to be laid for a pure and spiritual life, therefore, is that the virgin recognize her strengths. She will be able to exercise them well once she realizes she has them. Showing a person that he can actually achieve what he desires provides the most effective incentives for the soul. Even in warfare, the best way to influence and encourage a soldier is to remind him of his own power.

The first way to form a judgment of the goodness of human nature is from God, its creator. He made the whole world and all the extremely good things in it. How much more excellent, then, did he make the human beings, for whose sake he established everything else. The goodness of humanity was indicated even before it was created when God prepared to form it in his image and likeness. Then he subjected all the animals to human beings. He established the human beings as masters over beasts which were much more powerful in their size, strength, or armament. In this he clearly declared how much more wonderfully he had made humanity. God wanted human beings to be surprised by the subjection of these more powerful animals to themselves and thereby understand the excellence of their own nature. Still, he did not leave human beings naked and defenseless, did not expose them to evil like weaklings. Though he was made without external armament, the human person was given the better interior weapons of reason and judgment. Thus, through the understanding and the force of mind in which he excelled the other animals, he alone was to acknowledge the creator of all. He was to use the same faculty to dominate the beasts and to serve God. The Lord wanted him to accomplish justice voluntarily rather than by coercion. He left him in the hand of his own counsel, therefore, and placed before him life and death, good and evil [Ecclus. 15:14–16]. Whichever he chose would be given to him. Thus we read in Deuteronomy: "I have set life and death before your face, blessing and a curse. Choose life that you may live" [Deut. 30:19].

(3) We must be careful here that you are not disturbed by what tends to upset the ignorant crowd. You should not think that humanity was not created truly good because it is capable of evil and the impetuosity of nature is not bound by necessity to unchangeable good. If you consider the matter more carefully and force your mind to a deeper understanding of it, you will realize that what seems to count against it actually makes the human condition better and superior. The glory of the reasonable soul is located precisely in its having to face a parting of the ways, in its freedom to follow either path. I contend that the dignity of our nature consists entirely in this: this is the source of honor, of reward, of the praise merited by the best people. If a person could not go over to evil, he would not practice virtue in holding to the good. God decided to give rational creatures the gift of good will and the power of free choice. By making a person naturally capable of good and evil, so that he could do both and would direct his own will to either, God arranged that what an individual actually chose would be properly his own. The good could be done voluntarily only by a creature which was also capable of evil. Therefore the most excellent creator decided to make us capable of both.

Actually, of course, he intended and commanded that we should do what is good. His only purpose in giving the capacity for evil was that we accomplish his will by our own will. Our ability to do evil is, therefore, itself a good. I claim it is good because it makes its counterpart, the capacity for doing good, better. It removes the bonds of necessity and makes the person free to decide, makes the will voluntary in its own right. Thus we have the freedom to choose or oppose, to accept or reject. Every other creature has only the goodness which comes from its nature and condition; the reasonable being excels them all in having the goodness of its own will.

Still, many people consider the human condition and criticize the Lord's work by asserting with no less stupidity than irreverence that humanity should have been made incapable of doing evil. Thus the product says to his producer, "Why did you make me like this?" [Rom. 9:20]. These wicked people pretend that they do a good job of using what they were given and complain that they were not created differently. Instead of amending their lives, they want an improvement of their nature. Yet the goodness of nature was so universally established that it sometimes manifests itself even among the Gentiles who do not worship God. How many philosophers have we read or heard about or even seen ourselves who are chaste, patient, temperate, generous, restrained, and kind, who reject the honors as well as the pleasures of this world, who love justice as much as wisdom? Why are these virtues attractive to people who are themselves separated from God? Where did they get these good qualities if not from the goodness of nature? These values can be found either all together in the same person or singly in different individuals. Since all these people have the same nature' their examples show that not only what occurs in the whole group, but whatever occurs in any individual, could actually all be found, each and all, in every one. If, then, even apart from God, these people demonstrate how God made them, we should recognize what can be accomplished by Christians whose nature has been restored to a better condition by Christ and who are assisted by divine grace.

(4) Let us turn now to the secret depths of our souls and each reflect carefully on ourselves. What do our own feelings reveal to us? Let us attend to the testimony of a good conscience and be instructed by the authority within us. Indeed, we should learn its goodness from the mind itself rather than from somewhere else. What do we fear, what makes us ashamed whenever we sin? We give away our guilt by blushing or paleness. Our own conscience torments us even when

our anxious mind escapes detection for some little fault. When we do good, in contrast, we are joyful, at ease, and untroubled. If the good deed is secret, we wish people knew about it. Our nature reveals itself in these reactions: it manifests its goodness in turning away from evil deeds; it indicates what is appropriate for it when it relies on good works alone. The torments of a guilty conscience rage even in an undiscovered assassin; the mind's secret punishment tracks down the hidden criminal. The sinner cannot escape the penalty of his own guilt. Even if he is tortured, however, the innocent enjoys the security of a clear conscience. Although he fears the punishment itself, he is proud of his innocence.

Our souls possess what might be called a sort of natural integrity which presides in the depths of the soul and passes judgments of good and evil. As it approves upright and proper actions, so it condemns perverse works. According to the testimony of the conscience, by a kind of interior law, it distinguishes between the different deeds. It does not deceive us by contrived or clever rationalizations; rather, it uses the most faithful and incorruptible testimony of our own feelings to accuse or defend us. In writing to the Romans, the Apostle refers to this law and asserts that it is implanted in every person, written on the tablet of the heart. "The nations who do not have the law do what the law commands naturally. Although they do not possess this kind of law, they are a law unto themselves. They show that the book of the law is written on their hearts. Their conscience gives testimony, and their feelings either accuse or defend them" [Rom. 2:14–15]. Everyone who lived well and pleased God between the time of Adam and that of Moses actually made use of this law. I think it would be good for you to reflect on some of these holy people as examples. Once you realize how nature itself taught justice in place of the law, you will easily understand how good it is.

(5) Abel was the first to follow this teaching. He was deserving in God's eyes, so that the sacrifice he offered was pleasing to God. Its acceptance incited his brother to envy

[Gen. 4:4–7]. In the gospel, the Lord himself called him a just man and spoke of his perfection [Matt. 23:35]. This term "justice" includes all the forms of virtue. Similarly, we read that the Lord was so pleased with the blessed Enoch that he spirited him off from this mortal world. He was removed from this world once he had been perfected in it [Gen. 5:24]. Noah is also described as just and perfect in his generation. His holiness is all the more outstanding because when the whole world had deserted justice he alone remained upright. Rather than looking to anyone else, he provided an example of holiness. Thus, as the world approached shipwreck, he alone deserved to be told, "Enter the ark with your whole family because in this generation I have seen that you are just in my sight" [Gen. 7:1]. To be just in God's sight, a person must be pure in both body and heart. Melchizedek is called a priest of God [Gen. 14:18]. We can judge his merit by his foreshadowing the Lord's sacrament, which was to follow much later: he represented the mystery of the body and blood of Christ by the sacrifice of bread and wine. In the type of his priesthood, he symbolized that of Christ, to whom the Father said, "You are a priest forever, according to the order of Melchizedek" [Ps. 110:4]. When he blessed the chief of the patriarchs, Abraham, who is father of the Jews through circumcision and of the Gentiles through faith, he clearly portrayed the figure of the one who blessed both Jew and Gentile through his faith. The blessed Noah's virtue was also imitated by Lot: faced with the examples of so many sinners, he did not abandon justice. The example of the whole world did not overcome Noah; similarly, when his whole region was sinning, Lot maintained his integrity against the vices of the mob. As blessed Peter says, "He was upright in what he saw and heard" [2 Pet. 2:8]. Although he lived among the most wicked people, he shut his eyes and ears to their evil deeds. Thus God rescued Lot from the fire just as he had saved Noah from the flood.

What can I say about Abraham, the friend of God, or about Isaac or Jacob? God bestowed on them the extraordinary honor of naming himself their God, thus making himself part of their family. "I am the God of Abraham, the God of Isaac, the God of Jacob. This is my name forever, a memorial from generation to generation" [Exod. 3:15]. Thence we can judge how completely they did God's will. Joseph was the Lord's faithful servant from his youth, and each of his trials proved him more perfect and just. First his brothers handed him over to the Ishmaelites; those he had dreamed would honor him actually sold him [Gen. 37:5–10, 28]. He preserved the natural dignity of his spirit even when an Egyptian master acquired him. His example taught that slavery or freedom is a matter of sin or righteousness, that a person's own mind rather than his station counts against him. I ask you, virgin, to stop for a moment and carefully consider this chaste soul. When his master's wife desired the young Joseph, he remained unmoved. She approached and he fled. In everything else she simply commanded, but now she coaxed and pleaded. Neither his own youth nor the status of his lover prevailed on this chaste spirit. After he had often refused her, his mistress devised a trap for him. In secret and in private, she took his hand; with shameless entreaties she drew him to the adultery. He was not conquered. As he had met her words with words, he replied to her action with his own. When she asked, he refused; when she took hold of him, he ran away [Gen. 39:6–12]. Before the pronouncing of the gospel statement, "Whoever looks upon a woman with desire has already committed adultery with her in his heart" [Matt. 5:28], Joseph was challenged, not simply by a woman's figure, but practically by her very embrace; and still he did not desire her. You have been amazed by his chastity; you should also notice his kindness. Before the prophet had said, "No one shall hold malice against his neighbor in his heart" [Lev. 19:18], he answered hatred with love. When he saw those brothers who were actually more like enemies, he let his sorrow manifest his love and thus identify him to them. "He kissed each of them and threw himself upon their terrified necks. He wet them with his weeping. The tears of his love washed away his brother's hatred" [Gen. 45:15]. He always showed them a brotherly love, both while his father was alive and even after his death. He did not mention the pit into which they had thrown him to die. Nor did he brood over the brotherhood they had sold for a price. He responded to evil with good, thus fulfilling the Apostle's precept even when he was still under the law of nature [Rom. 12:17].

(6) What can I say about that celebrated athlete of God, the blessed Job? After his wealth was plundered, after his family property was destroyed, after his sons and daughters were all suddenly killed, he finally struggled against the devil in his own body. Every piece of property he owned was taken away, and all his abundant possessions suddenly fell away so that those goods which were truly his own would be clearly manifest. Everything was stripped away like clothing so that he would be stronger and freer to gain his victory, so that by enduring these sufferings he could a second time defeat the enemy he had already overcome by bearing the losses. The Lord himself honored him: "Have you overlooked my servant Job? No one on earth is like him, blameless, a true worshiper of God who refrains from all evil" [Job 2:3]. Nor was such praise undeserved. As Job says himself, he always feared the Lord who was like a sea crashing over him, a presence whose might he could not bear [Job 31:23]. He never dared despise the Lord he believed was present always. He said, "I am secure; my heart does not accuse me because of anything in my life" [Job 27:6]. Before the Lord had commanded us to love our enemies, he could say, "If I have enjoyed my enemy's misfortune, if I have said in my heart, 'well done' " [Job 31:29]. The gospel had not yet proclaimed, "Give to whoever asks of you" [Matt. 5:42], but Job had already stated, "If I have allowed the destitute to leave my house empty-handed" [Job 31:32]. He had not read the Apostle's direction "Masters, be just and fair to your slaves" [Col. 4:1]; yet he proclaimed to the Lord with assurance, "If I have injured a servant or harmed a maid, you know it Lord" [Job 31:13]. Before the same Apostle forbade the rich to be

haughty or to trust in uncertain riches [1 Tim. 6:17], he possessed his wealth in a way that showed his riches were elsewhere. "I did not trust in jewels or riches," he said [Job 31:24]. He proved this in deeds, not just in words. He did not grieve when he lost everything; instead he repeated in each instance, "The Lord gave; the Lord has taken away. Everything has happened as the Lord decided; blessed be the Lord's name forever. Naked I came forth from my mother's womb; naked shall I return" [Job 1:21]. We discover our true attitude toward some possession when we lose it; the desire to enjoy results in the pain of loss. When a person suffers no pain in losing something, he shows how he possessed it. Job was a man of the gospel even before the gospel, an apostolic man before the apostolic teaching. This disciple of the apostles opened up the hidden riches of nature, bringing them out of his own person and showing what all of us can accomplish. He taught how great is that endowment of the soul which we have but do not use. We refuse to demonstrate this goodness ourselves and then think we do not have it.

(7) We have spoken much about nature, and through the examples of the saints have illustrated and proven its goodness. Someone might try to reverse the argument and assert that the wickedness of some people shows that the blame falls upon nature itself. To block such a response, I will use the scriptural evidence which holds sinners responsible for the evil actions of the will and does not excuse them through some natural determinism. We read in Genesis, "The brothers Simeon and Levi accomplished their evil by their own will" [Gen. 49:5–6]. The Lord addressed Jerusalem, "Therefore they abandoned my way which I set before them. They did not heed my voice but went off after the will of their evil heart" [Jer. 9:13–14]. Again the same prophet says, "You sinned against God and did not pay attention to his voice. You refused to walk in his commands, his precepts, and his directives" [Jer. 44:23]. The Lord said through the prophet Isaiah, "If you decide to hear me, you will eat the good things of the earth. If you refuse and do not listen to

me, the sword will eat you" [Isa. 1:19–20]. Similarly, "A slaughter will cut all of you down because I called you and you did not listen; I spoke to you and you did not pay attention. You did what was evil in my sight and chose what I forbade" [Isa. 65:12]. The Lord himself says in the Gospel, "Jerusalem, Jerusalem, you kill the prophets and stone those sent to you. How often I have desired to gather your children as a hen gathers her chicks under her wings. But you refused" [Matt. 23:37]. Where we see willing and refusing, choosing and rejecting, we understand the functioning of freedom of the will, not the forces of nature. The books of both Testaments are full of similar passages which always describe good and evil as voluntary. For the sake of brevity we have to omit them. Since you are devoted to sacred reading, you will drink more deeply from the spring itself.

(8) We do not defend the goodness of nature by maintaining that it can do no wrong. Certainly we acknowledge that it is capable of both good and evil. We do, however, refute the charge that nature's inadequacy forces us to do evil. We do either good or evil only by our own will; since we always remain capable of both, we are always free to do either. Why should it be that some will judge and others be judged unless different choices occur in the same nature, unless we actually do different things when we could all do the same? Again, examples will clarify this point. Adam was driven from paradise; Enoch was delivered from this world. In each case the Lord showed the freedom of choice: as the sinner could have done well, so the saint could have done ill. Unless each could have done both, neither would the former have deserved to be punished nor the latter to be chosen by a just God. The cases of Cain and Abel, and of the twins Esau and Jacob, must be understood in the same way. We must realize that only the will causes different merits in the same nature. The world which was destroyed in the flood because of its sins was convicted by the upright Noah. Lot's integrity condemned the impurity of the Sodomites.

The fact that these early people lived for so many years

without the guidance of the law provides a significant proof of the goodness of human nature. God did not neglect his creation; he knew that human nature as he had made it was quite adequate as a law for them to practice justice. Thus, as long as the exercise of the recently created nature continued to thrive and the long practice of sinning had not shrouded human reason like a fog, nature was left without a law. Once it had been covered over by vices and corroded by the rust of ignorance, the Lord applied the law like a file to polish nature by repeated correction and restore its original luster. Doing good has become difficult for us only because of the long custom of sinning, which begins to infect us even in our childhood. Over the years it gradually corrupts us, building an addiction and then holding us bound with what seems like the force of nature itself. All the years during which we were negligently reared and were trained in the vices, during which we even labored at evil, during which the attractions of wickedness made innocence seem foolish, all these years now rise up against us. They come out against us, and the old practice battles the new decision. After we have labored so long to learn wickedness, are we then surprised that sanctity is not mysteriously bestowed upon us while we remain idle and at ease without working to build good customs?

We have mentioned these points about the goodness of nature briefly, as we have in other writings. We repeated them here only in order to smooth the path to perfect righteousness, so that knowing that the road is neither rough nor impassible you could run along it more easily. If even before the law and long before the coming of our Lord and Savior, some people lived upright and holy lives, as we have said, we should believe all the more that we can do the same after his coming. Christ's grace has taught us and regenerated us as better persons. His blood has purged and cleansed us; his example spurred us to righteousness. We should be better than people who lived before the law, therefore, and better than people who lived under the law. As the Apostle says, "Sin will no longer rule in you. You are not under the law but under grace'' [Rom. 6:14].

*   *   *   *   *

(13) If therefore you want your way of life to correspond to the magnificence of your resolution, if you want to be united to God in all things, if you want to make the light and easy yoke of Christ even lighter and easier for yourself, then you must at this point especially devote your attention to the blessed life. Apply yourself now so that the glowing faith of your recent conversion is always warmed by a new earnestness, so that pious practices may easily take root during your early years. What you establish in the beginning will last, and the rest of your life will follow the pattern you set at the start. Thus here at the beginning you must plan for the end. Think of what you want to have become by the last day and try to be that now.

Custom will nourish either vice or virtue, and its power is greatest when it develops in people from their early years. For establishing a way of life, therefore, the initial years are most important. Because they are tender and supple, they are easily formed and directed by free decisions, though people generally simply accustom themselves to worldly pursuits. Seedlings, which are young and not firmly rooted, follow any direction and are easily bent one way or another. Thus what nature curves is easily straightened according to a gardener's judgment. Animals too are easy to tame at a young and tender age. The earlier they are broken from running around freely, the more easily their neck takes to the yoke and their mouth to the bit. Literary pursuits are better implanted in young minds. The first things established in the mind tend to be firmly embedded in a person's disposition. Now all this is of the utmost importance when it comes to leading a good life. As long as your age makes you flexible and your soul responds easily to guidance, good custom should be practiced and established by bearing the yoke. Your mind should be directed to the highest matters, and the practice of a holy life should penetrate deep into your soul. Then the soul will climb to the very pinnacle of perfection and will exercise a facility in good living which is grounded in well-established custom. The soul will be amazed by its own virtue and even come to think that what it has actually learned was inborn in it.

*   *   *   *   *

(15) You should not fail to take seriously commands that involve lesser matters. God has commanded the least just as much as the greater. Thus you insult the lawgiver himself when you make light of his commands. Blessed Paul proclaims this, "Do everything without complaint or question so that you may be, without guilt or reproach, pure children of God in the midst of a depraved and perverse people, among whom you shine as lights in this world" [Phil. 2:14–15].

(16) We should linger here for a moment, virgin, and in each word of the Apostle examine the precious pearls that should adorn the bride of Christ. "Do everything," he says. We should fulfill all God's commands, not exercise our own judgment to select some of them. Nor should we look down on any of his precepts as insignificant or unimportant tokens. In all of them we should see the majesty of the Master himself. If without complaint or questioning we always consider its author, then no precept of God can possibly seem unimportant. We notice that ordinary and undistinguished supervisors are openly despised by their servants; their least orders are refused right to their faces. This does not happen, however, with noble personages. The more powerful the lord, the more quick his servants are to obey; the more difficult his orders, the more eagerly they are accepted. Thus, people are so anxious to be ruled by a king, and so ready to obey his directives, that they even desire to be commanded. They consider themselves fortunate not only when they accomplish the task but even when they are considered worthy of the command. Serving a person of great dignity is even regarded as a privilege.

God himself, of eternal majesty, of indescribable and incomparable power, bestows on us the sacred writings with the venerable points of his precepts. We do not, however, immediately receive them with reverence and joy. We do not consider it a wonderful privilege to be ruled over by such a great and honorable power, especially when the lawgiver's objective is the profit of the governed rather than his own advantage. In fact, we act like lazy and insolent servants, talking back to our Lord in a contemptuous and slovenly way: "That is too hard, too difficult! We cannot do that! We are only human; our flesh is weak!" What insane stupidity! What impious arrogance! We accuse the Lord of all knowledge of being doubly ignorant. We assert that he does not understand what he made and does not realize what he commands. We imply that the creator of humanity has forgotten its weakness and imposes precepts which a human being cannot bear. At the same time, moreover, we impiously charge the just God with wickedness and the loving God with cruelty. First we complain that he commands the impossible; then we assume that he condemns people for things they cannot avoid. We portray God as working to condemn rather than save us, something it is sacrilegious even to suggest.

The Apostle, therefore, realizing that the Lord of justice and majesty does not command the impossible, shields us from the complaining that tends to break out when orders are unfair or the commander is not respected. Why do we refuse to face the issue? Why do we complain to the lawgiver about the weakness of nature? No one knows the extent of our power better than the one who gave us our strength. No one understands what we can do better than the one who endowed us with the capacity for virtue. The just one did not choose to command the impossible; nor did the loving one plan to condemn a person for what he could not avoid.

(17) He continues, "That you may be without guile or reproach, perfect in your way of life" [Phil. 2:15]. A single term is adequate to express this, one which God specifies in the choosing of a bishop. A life that incurs no reproach must be very carefully protected, very integral indeed. Who could

53

have greater integrity than someone who practices true simplicity by never holding one thing in his heart and communicating another in word or expression. "As pure children of God," he says. This is the strongest exhortation possible, for Scripture to call us the children of God. Who would not be embarrassed and ashamed to do something unworthy of such a father, to turn someone called a child of God into a slave of vice? Hence he adds, "That we may be without blame." Since God is the source of all justice, the guilt of sin has no place in his children. "In the midst of a depraved and perverse people." This means that even if an infinite multitude of sinners surround you and innumerable examples of the vices press upon you, still you should so remember your heavenly birth that although you live among evil people, you conquer every evil. "Among whom you shine like lights in this world." Again we read in the Gospel, "Then the upright will shine like the sun in the kingdom of their Father" [Matt. 13:43]. A life corresponds to its reward. Thus those who will receive the splendor of the sun then should already radiate a like brightness of justice, their holy deeds should illumine the blindness of unbelievers. This connects with the same Apostle's idea in writing to the Corinthians: "The splendor of the sun differs from the splendor of the moon, and from the splendor of the stars. Moreover, each star differs in splendor from the others. So will it be in the resurrection of the dead" [1 Cor. 15:41–42]. The many mansions in the kingdom of heaven differ according to the merits of individuals. As good works differ, so do their rewards. Thus a person will shine there in glory as he has shone here in holiness.

Apply the strength of your whole mind to achieving a full perfection of life now. Prepare a heavenly life for its heavenly reward. The virgin's holiness should shine for all like the most splendid star. The greatness of her future reward should be indicated by renewal of her life. The way to goodness will be easier for you since your soul does not have evil customs to hold it back. Nor need we fear that the vices will hinder your pursuit of virtue or that the sterile sowing of the devil will ruin Christ's harvest. If penance can restore even people who have nearly obliterated the goodness of nature by prolonged sinful practices, if they can change the direction of their lives and destroy one custom with another, if they can go from being the worst to being among the best, then how much more can you overcome the evils that have never overcome you. You need only drive the vices away, not drive them out. How much easier not to acquire them than to get rid of them once they are acquired.

V.

The Canons of the Council of Carthage, A.D. 418

In the twelfth year of the consulate of Honorius Augustus, on the Calends of May, at Carthage in the basilica of Faustus [1 May 418].

Bishop Aurelius, along with Donatianus of Teleptensus, the bishop of the primatial see of the province of Bizacena, and two hundred and three of their fellow bishops of the provinces of Bizacena, Sitifensian Mauretania, Tripoli, Numidia, Caesarian Mauretania, and Spain, sitting in council with the deacons in attendance.

(1) All gathered in the holy synod of the Church of Carthage agreed to condemn anyone who says that the first human being, Adam, had been made mortal so that, whether he sinned or not, he would die in the body, that is, that he would depart from the body by a natural necessity rather than by the merit of sin.

(2) They also agreed to condemn anyone who denies that newborn children should be baptized or says that they are baptized for the forgiveness of sins but that they derive no original sin from Adam, which is then cleansed by the washing of regeneration, with the result that in their cases they understand the formula of baptism for the forgiveness of sins as false rather than true.

The statement of the Apostle "Through one person sin entered the world, and through sin death, so that it passed to all human beings in which all have sinned" [Rom. 5:12] should be understood only as the Catholic Church spread throughout the world has always interpreted it. Because of this rule of faith, even children who have not yet been able to commit any sin themselves are truly baptized for the forgiveness of sins, so that what they have derived by generation may be cleansed in them by regeneration.

(3) They also agreed to condemn anyone who asserts that in saying "in my Father's house there are many mansions" [John 14:2] the Lord meant that in the kingdom of heaven there will be some intermediate or other happy dwelling place for children who have left this life without baptism, which is necessary to enter that heavenly kingdom which is eternal life.

For since the Lord says, "Unless a person has been born again of water and the Spirit, he will not enter the kingdom of heaven" [John 3:5], what Catholic questions that a person who has not merited being a co-heir of Christ will share the lot of the devil? A person who does not attain the right hand will certainly end up on the left.

(4) They also agreed to condemn anyone who says that the grace of God which justifies us through our Lord Jesus Christ effects only the forgiveness of past sins but is not also a help not to commit sins.

(5) They also agreed to condemn anyone who says that the same grace of God through our Lord Jesus Christ helps us to avoid sinning only because it reveals and manifests to us an understanding of the commandments so that we know what to seek and to avoid, but that it does not also give us the desire and the strength actually to accomplish what we know we should.

Since the Apostle says, "Knowledge puffs up; charity builds up" [1 Cor. 8:1], it would be quite irreverent for us to believe that we have the grace of Christ for what puffs up but not for what builds up, since God gives us the good and true gift both of knowing what we should do and of desiring to do it, so that when charity builds up, knowledge cannot puff up. Thus, as it is written of God, "who teaches human beings knowledge" [Ps. 94:10], it is also written, "Charity is from God" [1 John 4:7].

(6) They also agreed to condemn anyone who says that the grace of justification is given that we may more easily fulfill through grace what we are commanded to accomplish through free choice, as though we could still fulfill the divine commands, though not as easily, even if grace were not given.

When he spoke about the observance of the commandments, the Lord said not "Without me you can do only with great difficulty," but "Without me you can do nothing" [John 15:5].

(7) They also agreed to condemn anyone who interprets the statement of the holy Apostle John "If we say that we are without sin, we deceive ourselves and truth is not in us" [1 John 1:8] as meaning that for the sake of humility we should not declare ourselves free of sin, not because this is the way things really are.

The apostle continues and adds, "If however we confess our sins, the one who is faithful and just will forgive our sins and cleanse us from all iniquity" [1 John 1:9]. Here it is obvious that he means this not only in humility but in truth. This apostle could have said, "If we say that we have no sin, we boast and humility is not in us." But since he said, "We deceive ourselves and truth is not in us" [1 John 1:8], it is obvious that a person who claims he has no sin asserts a falsehood, not the truth.

(8) They also agreed to condemn anyone who says that in the Lord's Prayer the saints say, "Forgive us our debts," not to make this petition for themselves, since it is no longer necessary in their own case, but for the sake of others among their people who are sinners. Thus no one of the saints would say, "Forgive me my debts," but only, "Forgive us our debts," so that the just person is understood to be praying for others more than for himself.

The Apostle James was holy and just when he said, "We all offend in many ways" [James 3:2]. The only reason the

"all" was included was to bring the statement into agreement with the psalm, where we read, "Do not enter into
judgment with your servant, since no one living will be
justified in your sight" [Ps. 143:2]; and with the prayer of the
most wise Solomon "There is no one who has not sinned" [2
Chron. 6:36]; and with the book of the holy Job "He seals up
the hand of everyone so that each may know his weakness"
[Job 37:7]. Thus even the holy and just Daniel spoke in the
plural in his prayer, "We have sinned; we have done iniquity" [Dan. 9:5], and in the other things he confesses there, not
through humility but in truth. And lest anyone think, as
some indeed have, that he was referring to the sins of his people rather than his own, he said later, "When I prayed and
confessed my sins and the sins of my people to the Lord my
God" [Dan. 9:20]. He did not choose to say, "our sins," but
both those of the people and his own, because as a prophet he
foresaw those who would understand the matter so wrongly.

(9) They also agreed to condemn anyone who interprets the
words of the Lord's Prayer "Forgive us our debts" as spoken
by the saints in humility rather than in truth.

Who can tolerate a person who in his very praying lies not
to human beings but to the Lord himself by saying with his
mouth that he wants to be forgiven and at the same time saying in his heart that he has no debts to be forgiven him?

VI.

Augustine

ON THE GRACE OF CHRIST

(I.1) My dearest friends Albina, Pinianus, and Melania, beloved of God, my joy in receiving word of your physical and even more spiritual well-being surpasses words. Since I could not express it anyway, let me leave it to your good thoughts and turn immediately to the matters about which you inquired. The messenger is in a hurry and I am always busier when I am in Carthage than anywhere else. Using the opportunities God has provided, however, I have written out what I could.

(II.2) You wrote to me that you had spoken to Pelagius and urged him to condemn in writing whatever charges are brought against him. You report that in your presence he replied, "I anathematize anyone who either thinks or says that the grace of God, 'by which Christ came into the world to save sinners' [1 Tim. 1:15], is not necessary, not only at every hour and moment, but in each of our acts. May anyone who tries to take away this grace suffer eternal punishment." Now anyone who heard this and did not also know his meaning, which he explains clearly enough in his books, would certainly think he believed the truth in this matter. The books to which I refer are neither those he claims were circulated before he had a chance to go over and correct them, nor the ones he denies he wrote at all. I am talking about those books mentioned in the letters he sent to Rome. A person who pays attention to the things he says openly in these writings should be cautious even about the statement you report. He could be understanding the grace of God, "by which Christ came into this world to save sinners," simply as the forgiveness of sins and intend his statement in this sense. He could say that the grace is necessary at every hour and moment and in each activity because, by recalling and remaining mindful that our sins had been forgiven, we would not sin again. Thus we could be helped not by God's supplying strength but by the energies of our own will which in each activity remembers the advantage provided by the forgiveness of sins. Similarly, they could give this statement another meaning, since they usually explain that Christ provided help for us to avoid sin because by his own just living and teaching he left an example. Thus they would say that grace is necessary for us in every moment and action in the sense that we must keep the example of the Lord's way of life before us in our daily lives. Your faith will perceive the difference between a confession of this sort and a proper acknowledgment of the grace in question. Yet that difference can be concealed by the ambiguity of the terms.

(III.3) Do not be surprised at this. Indeed, the same Pelagius made no protest when before an episcopal tribunal he condemned all who say that the grace of God is not given for individual acts but consists instead in free choice or in the law and teaching. At the same time, he also condemned those who teach that God's grace is given according to our merits. At that point we thought all his subterfuges were over. Yet in the book he published, *On Free Choice*, which he mentions in the letter sent to Rome, it became clear that his own position does not really differ from what he seemed to have condemned. God's grace and the assistance by which he helps us to avoid sin are located either in nature and free choice or in the law and teaching. Thus God would help a person to "turn from evil and do good"[1 Pet. 3:11] by showing and revealing what he should do, not also by co-operating with him and inspiring love so that he actually does what he realized he should.

(4) Pelagius sets down and distinguishes three elements

which he says are involved in fulfilling divine commands. capacity, will, and action. By his capacity a person can be just, by his will he decides to be just; by his action he is just. The first of these, capacity, is given by the creator of human nature and lies outside our power; we have it even against our own will. The other two, will and action, are ours, he claims; he attributes them to us as deriving only from ourselves. He then asserts that the grace of God helps not the two which he regards as our own, will and action, but rather the other, capacity, which comes from God and is not in our power. Will and action, which are our own, are strong enough to turn from evil and do good without divine aid. The capacity which we receive from God, however, is so weak that it is always assisted by the help of grace.

(IV.5) To prevent a countercharge that we have either not properly understood what he is saying or have maliciously interpreted his statements in a way he did not intend, we shall quote him directly. "Thus we distinguish these three and then divide them according to a definite sequence. In the first place we set capacity, second willing, and third being. We locate capacity in nature, willing in decision, and being in performance. The first, capacity, is properly related to God who endowed his creature with it. The other two, willing and being, should be referred to the human person because they derive from his own decision. Thus praise belongs to a person for his will and good works, or rather this praise belongs both to the person and to God, because God gave the capacity for the will and work, and because God always assists this capacity with the help of his grace. That a person can will and perform good derives from God alone. This first can exist without the other two, but the other two cannot occur without the first. Hence I am free to have neither good will nor good action, but I simply cannot exist without the capacity for good. This is in me even if I prefer not to have it. Nature never takes leave of itself in this regard. Some examples taken from our sense faculties will clarify this point. That our eyes can see is not our own; that we see well or ill is ours. That we can talk at all comes from God; that we speak well or ill comes from us. That we are able to think, speak, and do every good thing is from him who gave, from him who helps this capacity; that we either think or speak or act well, however, is our own, since we can also turn all three to evil. Now this point must be repeated often because of your malicious accusations. When we say that a person can be without sin, and by thus recognizing the capacity we have received, we praise God who endowed us with it, we are dealing with the work of God alone and offer no occasion for human praise. Here we are interested only in what is possible, not in either the willing or the being which follow.''

(V.6) Notice that these statements exactly express the whole position Pelagius takes in the third book of his treatise, *On Free Choice*. In that book he was concerned to distinguish these three very precisely: first to be able, second to will, third to be, that is, capacity, will, and action. Thus whenever we read or hear him acknowledge the help of the divine grace by which we avoid evil and accomplish good, whether he locates it in the law and teaching or anywhere else, we can understand what he is saying and not fall into the error of interpreting him in a way contrary to his views. We must realize that he believes that neither our will nor our action is helped by divine aid. He believes that such help is given only to the capacity to will and work, the only member of this trio which he says comes from God. Hence he believes that this capacity which God himself has placed in human nature is weak while the other two which he claims for us are so stable, strong, and self-sufficient that they do not need God's aid. Thus he believes that God does not help us to will, that he does not help us to act, that he helps us only to be able to will and to act.

The Apostle contradicts this when he says, "With fear and trembling work out your salvation" [Phil. 2:12]. He wanted them to realize that they were divinely assisted not only in being able to work, which they had already acquired in nature and by instruction, but also in their actual working. Thus he did not say, "God works in you to be able," as though they had willing and working of themselves and had no need of God's help for these two. Instead he said, "It is God who works in you both to will and to accomplish," or as other and especially the Greek manuscripts read, "both to will and to work" [Phil. 2:13]. You could suspect that by the help of the Holy Spirit the Apostle foresaw these future opponents of God's grace and therefore asserted that both to will and to work are actually caused in us by God. Yet Pelagius wants to make these two so much our own that they are not even assisted by the help of divine grace.

(VI.7) Pelagius deceived no one in this statement, not the unwary and simple, nor even himself. Once he had asserted, "A person is praised for his will and work," he corrected himself by adding, "indeed the praise belongs both to the person and to God." He did not say this, however, because he wanted to be sure that his readers understood the sound doctrine that God works in us both to will and to work. The specification which follows immediately makes his intention unmistakable, "who gave the capacity for will and work." From his preceding explanation, of course, it is clear that he located this capacity in nature itself. Rather than say nothing at all about grace, then, he tacked on "and who by the help of his grace always assists this capacity." If he had said "this will or this performance," he would not have appeared to hold back from the Apostolic teaching. Instead he said, "By the help of his grace, he always assists this capacity," thereby indicating that one of the trio which he located in nature. Thus, according to Pelagius, praise for willing and acting is due both God and the human person, but not because the person wills as God stirs up the fire of love in his will, or because the person works as God works within him. Yet what is a human being without God's help? Actually, Pelagius tacks on the praise of God because we would neither will nor act unless he had created us with a nature that makes us capable of willing and acting.

(8) Although he acknowledges that this natural capacity is helped by God's grace, it is not clear here either what kind of

grace he is talking about or how much he thinks it helps the nature. This passage can be understood, however, in the same way as the others where he expresses himself more fully. All he intends as aids to the natural capacity are the law and teaching.

(VII) Thus he says in one place, "At this point, people who are untrained in this matter think we slight divine grace because we say that this grace in no way completes holiness in us without our own will. It is not as though God commands something belonging to his grace and then does not provide the help of that grace to those he commanded, so that they might accomplish more easily through grace what they are commanded to do through free choice." Then, as though he were explaining what kind of grace he is talking about, he goes on to say, "Which grace we acknowledge not in law alone, as you think we do, but also in the assistance of God." Is there anyone who at this point would not want him to explain what kind of grace he means? Because he says here that he does not acknowledge grace in the law alone, we have every reason to expect him to expand this statement. But look at what he sets before our eager anticipation. "God helps us through his teaching and revelation when he opens the eyes of our hearts, when he shows us the things to come lest we become preoccupied with those at hand, when he lays bare the traps of the devil, when he enlightens us by the manifold and ineffable gift of heavenly grace." Then he concludes his exposition with a sort of self-acquittal. "Would you think a person who says such things seems to deny divine grace or that he actually recognizes both human freedom and God's grace?" In all of this he never gets beyond his commendation of the law and teaching. He diligently drives home his point that this is the assisting grace, and in this way elaborates what he set forth in saying, "But we acknowledge grace also in the assistance of God." He thought the help of God could be presented in a variety of ways by referring to teaching, revelation, the opening of the eyes of the heart, the showing of things to come, pointing out satanic snares, and enlightening by the manifold and ineffable gift of heavenly grace. The purpose of all such help, of course, is to make us learn the divine precepts and promises. All this is therefore only a locating of God's grace in the law and teaching!

(VIII.9) Here then it becomes evident that the grace Pelagius acknowledges is God's showing and revealing what we ought to do, not his giving and helping us to do it. Yet when the assistance of grace is missing, knowledge of the law is more effective in producing a violation of the commandment. "Where there is no law, neither is there transgression" [Rom. 4:15], says the Apostle; he then adds, "I would not have recognized lust unless the law had said, 'You shall not lust' " [Rom. 7:7]. Thus the law and grace are so different that the law is not only useless but actually an obstacle in many ways unless grace assists. This shows, moreover, the function of the law: it makes people guilty of transgression and forces them to take refuge in grace in order to be liberated and helped to overcome evil desires. It commands more than it helps; it diagnoses illness but does not cure. Indeed, far from healing the infirmity, the law actually makes it worse in order to move a person to seek the medicine of grace more anxiously and insistently, because "the letter kills but the spirit gives life" [2 Cor. 3:6]. "If a law had been given which could give life, then righteousness certainly would come from the law" [Gal. 3:21]. To indicate what help the law does give, however, Paul adds, "The Scripture shut up everything under sin so that the promise might be given to believers from faith in Jesus Christ. The law, therefore, was our guide to Christ Jesus" [Gal. 3:22, 24]. Being strictly and undeniably shut up under sin is good for a proud person, since it prevents his trusting in the strength of free choice to accomplish righteousness. Thus: "But that every mouth may be shut and every pure person become guilty before God, since all flesh shall not be justified before him from the law. Through the law comes the knowledge of sin. Now, however, the righteousness of God which was made known through the law and the prophets has been exhibited without the law"

[Rom. 3:19–21]. If it was made known through the law, how is righteousness exhibited without the law? Not that it is exhibited without the law but that it is righteousness without the law because it is God's righteousness, that righteousness which comes to us not from the law but from God. It is not the righteousness we recognize and cringe before when God commands but that which we love and cling to when he gives it, so that "whoever glories may glory in the Lord" [1 Cor. 1:31].

(IX.10) What then is the point of Pelagius' specifying the law and teaching as that grace which helps us to work righteousness, since the only help they provide is in moving us to seek grace? No one can fulfill the law through the law itself, since "the fullness of the law is love" [Rom. 13:10] and "the love of God is shed abroad in our hearts," not through the law but "through the Holy Spirit who is given to us" [Rom. 5:5]. Further, grace is pointed out through the law, so that the law may be fulfilled through grace.

Of what advantage is it to Pelagius, then, to keep saying the same thing over again in different words in order to prevent people from realizing that the grace which he insists helps the capacity of nature actually consists in the law and teaching? As far as I can tell, he is afraid this will be understood because he condemned those who say that God's grace and help are not given for individual acts but consist in free choice or in the law and teaching. Yet he thinks he escapes detection when in a great variety of circumlocutions he deals with this same notion of law and teaching.

(X.11) In another passage, after a long declaration that our own effort rather than God's help produces good will in us, Pelagius posed a question to himself from an epistle of the Apostle. "How then will the Apostle's statement be true, 'It is God who works in you both to will and to accomplish' [Phil. 2:13]?" In order to answer this objection, which he realized was diametrically opposed to his position, he then added, "He works in us to will what is good, to will what is holy. We have given ourselves over to earthly desire and like dumb animals love only the things around us; then he inflames us with the greatness of the glory to come and the promise of rewards; then he rouses the sluggish will to a desire for God by a revelation of wisdom; then he urges us to all that is good." It should be noted that he does not hesitate to deny this last part elsewhere. But how could it be more evident that in speaking of that grace by which God works in us to will what is good, what he really means is the law and instruction? The greatness of the coming glory and of the rewards is promised in the law and the teaching of the Holy Scriptures. The revealing of wisdom is a form of teaching. Urging all that is good is likewise a type of instruction. If indeed there be any difference between teaching and urging, or rather exhorting, then this too falls under the title of instruction, which is given in some type of speaking or writing. Thus even the Holy Scriptures both teach and exhort. Further, human action can have a role in both teaching and exhorting. We wish, however, they would occasionally acknowledge that grace by which the greatness of the glory to come is not only promised but also believed in and hoped for, by which wisdom is not only revealed but also loved, by which all that is good is not only urged but actually prevails as well. "Not everyone has faith" [2 Thess. 3:2], even of those who hear the Lord promising the kingdom of heaven through the Scriptures. Nor is everyone who is urged actually persuaded to come to him who says, "Come to me all who labor" [Matt. 11:28]. He himself indicated well enough who has faith and who is persuaded to come to him when he says, "No one comes to me unless the Father who sent me has drawn him" [John 6:44], and a bit later when speaking of nonbelievers, "I said to you that no one can come to me unless my Father has given this to him" [John 6:65]. This is the grace Pelagius must confess if he wants not only to bear the name but really to be a Christian.

(XI.12) What shall I say about the revelation of wisdom? Will anyone naively hope to attain in this life the greatness of the revelations given to the Apostle Paul? Or should we suppose that what was revealed to him was something other than wisdom? Yet Paul says, "Lest I be puffed up by the greatness of my revelations, a torment of my flesh was given me, an agent of Satan who harassed me. Three times I asked the Lord to rid me of it. He said to me, 'My grace is enough for you, for power is perfected in weakness' " [2 Cor. 12:7–9]. Can there be any doubt that this agent of Satan, whose beatings suppressed the pride which could have arisen because of the greatness of the revelations, would have been unnecessary if the Apostle had already possessed that greatest and fullest charity which cannot be puffed up? The characterization of charity which says, "Charity is not competitive, is not puffed up" [1 Cor. 13:4] is certainly accurate. Charity went on growing daily even in such an apostle, as long as his interior self was being renewed from day to day [2 Cor. 4:16], to be perfected until it was beyond being puffed up. Until this solid structure of charity was completed, however, his mind would still have been puffed up by the greatness of the revelations. He had set out but not yet arrived; he ran but had not yet won.

(XII.13) If a person is unwilling to endure the troubles that suppress his pride before charity reaches its full and final perfection in him, then the admonition "My grace is enough for you, for power is perfected in weakness" [2 Cor. 12:9] is properly addressed to him. The weakness is not of the flesh alone, as Pelagius thinks, but is of both the flesh and the soul. At the time when it would have been exalted, Paul's soul was still weak in comparison to its full perfection. Further, the agent of Satan was described as sent to torment the flesh, even though Paul's was quite solid in comparison to the flesh of carnal and passionate people who do not discern "what comes from the Spirit of God" [1 Cor. 2:14]. Therefore, if power is perfected in weakness, anyone who does not acknowledge his weakness is not perfected. That grace by which "power is perfected in weakness" leads to the highest perfection and glorification for those who are predestined and called according to purpose. By this grace, God not only makes us know what we should do but do what we know, not only believe what we should love but love what we believe.

(XIII.14) If this grace is to be explained as instruction, this must be so qualified that we believe that God bestows it more deeply and interiorly with an unspeakable sweetness, that he imparts it not simply through those who plant and water from the outside but secretly nurtures the growth himself [1 Cor. 3:7], that he not only manifests truth but gives charity. This is the way God teaches those he has called according to purpose, giving them at the same time both to know what to do and to do what they know. Thus the Apostle says to the Thessalonians, "You do not need me to write to you about charity, since you have yourselves learned from God to love one another" [1 Thess. 4:9]. Moreover, to show that they had learned it from God himself, he added, "Indeed, you do this for the brethren in the whole of Macedonia" [1 Thess. 4:10]. Thus a person's doing what he learns is the surest sign that he learned it from God. In this way all those called according to purpose are "taught by God" [Isa. 54:13], as is written in the prophets. Those, however, who knew what they should do and do not do it have learned from God not by grace but by the law, not according to the Spirit but according to the letter.

Still, many seem to do what the law commands out of fear of punishment rather than love of justice. The Apostle calls this their own justice, which comes from the law as something commanded rather than given. When it is given, justice is not called ours but God's, because it comes to us from God. Thus he says, "That I may be found in him not having my own justice which comes from the law but that which comes from faith in Jesus, justice from God" [Phil. 3:9]. Law and grace are so different that, although there is no doubt that the law comes from God, still the righteousness which comes from the law is not from God, while the righteousness perfected through grace is from God. The righteousness which is maintained because of the law's curse is attributed to the law; the righteousness attributed to God comes through the blessing of grace which makes the command attractive rather than threatening. Thus the Psalmist prays, "Lord you are sweet; in your sweetness teach me your righteousness" [Ps. 119:68]. He asks not to be coerced by servile fear of punishment under the law, but to enjoy working by free love with the law. To fulfill a precept willingly is to do it freely. Whoever learns in this way actually accomplishes whatever he has learned should be done.

(XIV.15) The Lord describes this type of teaching when he says, "Everyone who has heard and learned from my Father comes to me" [John 6:45]. Thus, if a person does not come, it cannot be said that "he heard and learned he should come" but did not choose to do what he had learned. This simply cannot be accurately said about that kind of instruction in which God teaches by grace. If, indeed, according to Truth himself, "Anyone who has learned, comes," then whoever does not come certainly has not learned. Who does not realize that a person comes or does not come by his free choice? If he does not come, then free choice acted alone. If he comes, however, then it must have been helped, and helped not only to know what to do but to do what it knows. Thus when God teaches through the grace of the Spirit rather than the letter of the law, the result of his teaching is not simply that a person is aware of what he has learned by knowing but also that he seeks it by willing and accomplishes it by acting. This divine way of teaching assists not only the natural capacity for willing and working but also the actual willing and working itself. If this grace helped only our capacity, the Lord would have said, "Everyone who has heard and learned from the Father can come to me." This, however, is not what he said, but instead, "Everyone who has heard and learned from the Father comes to me." Pelagius locates this capacity to come in nature, or even, as he has begun to say recently, in that grace "by which the capacity is aided"—whatever his notion of this might be. He still locates coming itself in the willing and working. Yet it does not follow that a person who can come actually does come unless he wills and accomplishes it. Everyone, however, who learns from the Father not only can come, but actually does come. Here, the actualization of the capacity, the movement of the will, and the achievement of the operation are found together.

(XV.16) What then was the point of Pelagius' examples unless they actually clarified his position, as he promised they would? Hence we should examine them not to agree with them but in order to use them to understand what he thinks more clearly and exactly. He says: "That our eyes can see is not ours. But it is ours to see well or ill." Let the prayer of the psalm respond to this: "Turn away my eyes, lest they look upon vanity" [Ps. 119:37]. Even if the reference is to the eyes of the mind, seeing well or ill begins there and extends to the eyes of the body. Seeing well or ill refers here not to sharp or blurred vision but to the good regard which assists or the evil regard which lusts. Through the outer eyes one sees a beggar to help or a woman to desire, but the mercy or lust of good or evil sight comes from the inner eyes. Why then do we say to God, "Turn away my eyes lest they look upon vanity?" [Ps. 119:37]. If God does not assist the will itself, why do we ask him for what is in our own power?

(XVI.17) Pelagius says, "Our power to speak comes from God, but it is ours to speak well or ill." This is not what the Good Speaker teaches: "It is not you who speak, but the Spirit of your Father who speaks in you" [Matt. 10:20]. Yet Pelagius asserts, "I would generalize to cover every instance. Our power to think, speak, and accomplish any good is of him who gave this capacity, who assists this power." Notice that he repeats here his earlier view that of the trio—capacity, will, and action—only the capacity is assisted. Then to complete his thought he adds, "Our actual thinking, speaking, or doing well is, however, our own." This time he even forgot the kind of correction he had included earlier. When he said, "A person is praised for good will and work," he added, "Indeed, both the person and God who gave the capacity to will and work." Why did he not repeat this in giving his examples, so that he might at least have said in concluding, "Our power to think, speak, and accomplish any good is of him who gave this capacity, who helps this power. Our actual thinking, speaking, or acting is both ours and his"? He did not say this, however, and unless I am mistaken I think I see why he was afraid to do so.

(XVII.18) When he comes to show why these activities are ours he says, "Because we can turn them all to evil." He refrained from affirming that they are "ours and God's," because he was afraid that his assertion would be turned against him. If our good thinking, speaking, and acting were ours and God's because he gave us this capacity, then our evil thinking, speaking, and action would also be ours and God's because he gave us the capacity for both. Thus just as we would be praised with God for good works, we should also be blamed along with him for evil. This, however, is inadmissible. Yet the capacity God gave us makes us just as capable of doing evil as good.

(XVIII.19) This is the way Pelagius describes this capacity in the first book of the treatise, *On Free Choice*: "We have the capacity for either direction implanted in us by God as a sort of fertile and fruitful root. By the human will this root produces and bears different fruits. According to its cultivator's decision, it can either bloom with the flowers of virtue or bristle with the thorns of vice." He did not realize what he was saying here when, in opposition to the truth of the Gospels and the teachings of the apostles, he assigned the same root to both good and evil works. The Lord said neither that a good tree can bear evil fruit nor that an evil tree could produce good [Matt. 7:18]. Similarly, when the Apostle Paul identifies cupidity as the root of all evil [1 Tim. 6:10], he implies that charity should be recognized as the root of all good. Thus, if these two trees are two persons, one good and the other evil, then would it not follow that the good person is the one of good will, the tree with the good root, and the evil person is the one of bad will, the tree with the evil root? Thus the fruits of these two roots and trees are the good thoughts, words, and deeds which come from the good will, and the evil ones which come from the bad will.

(XIX.20) A person becomes a good tree when he receives God's grace. He does not change himself from evil into good by his own resources; rather this is effected from him and through him and in him who is always good. This same grace is necessary not only to make the tree good, but also to help it bear good fruit. Without it a person can do nothing good. Thus, God works along with good trees to produce their fruit. He waters and cultivates from the outside through a minister, and he himself gives growth within [1 Cor. 3:7].

A person becomes an evil tree when he makes himself evil, when he turns away from the unchangeable good. This defection from good is the source of bad will. Rather than introducing a different, evil nature, the defect corrupts the nature that was created good. Thus, when the injury is healed no evil remains, because the corruption was in the nature but was not identified with it.

(XX.21) The capacity itself then is not one and the same root of both good and evil, as he [Pelagius] thinks. Charity is the root of good; cupidity is the root of evil [1 Tim. 6:10]; they differ as virtue and vice. The capacity itself, of course, can admit either of these roots: a person can have not only the charity which makes him a good tree but also the cupidity which makes him an evil one. A person's cupidity, which is a defect, is originated either by a human person or by humanity's deceiver, but not by humanity's creator. This is indeed "the concupiscence of the flesh and the concupiscence of the eyes and the ambition of this age, which is not from the Father but from the world" [1 John 2:16]. The scriptural term "the world" refers, as everyone knows, to the inhabitants of this world.

(XXI.22) According to scriptural witness, we have charity, which is a virtue, not from ourselves but from God. "Charity is from God, and everyone who loves is born of God and knows God, because God is charity" [1 John 4:7, 8]. The text "The one born of God does not sin because he cannot sin" [1

John 3:9] is best interpreted through this charity, because the charity by which he is born of God "does not act falsely, nor does it plot evil" [1 Cor. 13:5]. Thus a person who sins does not act according to charity; rather, he follows the cupidity by which he is not born of God. As we have said, the capacity itself can have both of these roots. When Scripture says, "Charity is from God," or, more strongly, "God is charity" [1 John 4:7, 8]; when the Apostle John insistently asserts, "See the charity which the Father has given us so that we may be called and indeed be children of God" [1 John 3:1]; when he hears, "God is charity" [1 John 4:8]; why does Pelagius continue to maintain that of that trio we have only the capacity from God, the will and good action from ourselves? Good will is nothing else but charity which, as Scripture proclaims, is ours from God, given by the Father to make us his children.

(XXII.23) Perhaps, however, our prior merits gain charity for us, as Pelagius thinks of God's grace in the treatise he addressed to a consecrated virgin, the one he mentions in his letters to Rome. Citing the statement of the Apostle James which says, "Submit to God, resist the devil, and he will flee from you" [James 4:7], Pelagius continues, "He shows how we should resist the devil. If we submit to God and earn divine grace by doing his will, then with the help of the Holy Spirit we may more easily resist the evil spirit." [*To Demetrias* 25.] Judge for yourselves his good faith when, during that church trial in Palestine, he condemned those who say that the grace of God is given according to our merits. Can we still doubt that he continues to hold and openly preach just this? How then was his confession in the episcopal hearing truthful? Had he perhaps already written this treatise in which he expressly states the thesis he then condemned without any protest in the eastern synod? In that case, he should have admitted that he had once held this but had given it up, so that we could unhesitatingly rejoice in his progress. Later, however, when the charge was included among other objections posed to him, he replied, "Let those who assert that these are Caelestius' opinions look into the matter.

I have never held this, and I condemn all who do hold it."
[Augustine, *On the Proceedings Against Pelagius* xiv.30.]
How, indeed, could he never have held this if he had already
written the treatise? Or how could he condemn those who do
hold this if he then wrote the book afterward?

(24) Still, he might reply that he meant, "We earn divine
grace by doing God's will," in the sense that once they have
first received a grace to do God's will, further grace to oppose
the tempter resolutely is then given to those who are faithful
and live devoutly. Lest he attempt this kind of response, however, notice some of his other statements on this. He says,
"When a person runs to the Lord, seeks to be guided by him,
that is, joins his own will to the Lord's will and becomes one
spirit with him, as the Apostle says [1 Cor. 6:17], all this is
done only by freedom of choice." Look at what he claims is
accomplished only by freedom of choice. He judges that we
join ourselves to God without God's assistance. The meaning
of "only by freedom of choice" is that when we have joined
ourselves to him without his help, we then earn his help because we have already adhered to him.

(XXIII) He continues on the subject of those who use freedom of choice well: "One who uses it well surrenders himself
fully to God and mortifies his own will completely so that he
can say with the Apostle, 'It is not I who live now but Christ
who lives in me' [Gal. 2:20]. He places his heart in God's
hands so that he may direct it wherever he will" [Prov. 21:1].
That God would guide our heart wherever he wills is truly a
great help of divine grace. Pelagius foolishly thinks, however,
that we earn this great help when by freedom of choice alone
and without any help we run to the Lord, ask to be guided by
him, join our wills to his, and by adhering to him become
one spirit with him. In his view we accomplish all these enor-
mous good works by freedom of choice alone. Through these
preceding merits we attain the grace that God would direct
our hearts where he chooses.

How can this be grace when it is not given gratuitously?
How is it grace if it is paid as our due? How is the Apostle's

statement true, "This is not from you but is the grace of God; it is not from your achievements, lest anyone be puffed up" [Eph. 2:8, 9]? Or again when he says, "If it is from works, then it is not grace" [Rom. 11:6]? How can all this be true, I ask, if these great works precede and earn for us that merit of acquiring grace for which it would be paid as our due rather than gratuitously given? Would we run to God without his aid in order to attain his aid? Would we adhere to God without his help so that he would then help us as we cling to him? What greater or even comparable achievement could grace offer a person who has already managed without it, by freedom of choice alone, to become one spirit with the Lord?

(XXIV.25) I would like to hear Pelagius explain the case of that Assyrian king whose bed the holy woman Esther abhorred: "He was seated on the throne of his kingdom, robed in all his splendor, decked in marvelous hues with gold and precious stones, exceedingly awesome. Then lifting up his face, which was blazing in glory, he glared at her like an enraged bull in full charge. The queen was frightened; the color drained from her face, and she collapsed onto the maiden who went before her" [Esther 15:6, 7].

Now I wish Pelagius would tell us whether this king had already run to the Lord, had longed to be guided by him, had joined his will to God's, and in adhering to him had become one spirit with him only by freedom of choice; whether he had surrendered himself fully to God, mortified his will completely, and placed his heart in the hand of God. I believe a person would have to be crazy, not just stupid, to think this about the king as he was at that moment. And yet God changed and converted his rage into gentleness. Will anyone doubt that changing and converting this rage into the contrary gentleness is greater than turning in one direction a heart which is not caught up in either emotion, which is midway between them? Let them therefore read and understand, let them observe and acknowledge that not by the law and teaching which thunder outside, but by an internal and secret, a marvelous and indescribable power, God produces in human hearts not only true revelations but good wills.

(XXV.26) Let Pelagius therefore desist from deceiving both himself and others by arguing against the grace of God. God's graciousness to us must be proclaimed not only in the case of one member of that trio, the capacity for good willing and working, but in good will and operation as well. He specifies that this power is capable of both alternatives. He wants to attribute our good works to God because they come from this power; yet the sins which come from this same power should not be referred to God. Hence, the help of divine grace is to be recognized not simply because it assists the natural capacity.

Let Pelagius cease proclaiming, therefore, that we owe our power to think, speak, and do good to God who gave this power and helps it, but that we owe our performance in thinking, speaking, and doing well to ourselves. Enough of this! God not only gave our power and helps it; "he works in us to will and to work" [Phil. 2:13]. This is not because we ourselves do not actually will and work, but because we neither will nor perform any good without his assistance. How can he say, "Our power to act well is from God but our action is our own," when the Apostle says that he prays to God that those he addresses would do what is good and abstain from all evil? Thus Paul says, "We pray that you abstain from evil," not "that you may be able to abstain from evil" and "that you do good," not "that you may be able to do good" [2 Cor. 13:7]. Those described by "whoever is led by the Spirit of God is a child of God" [Rom. 8:14] are certainly led by him who is good to lead lives that are good.

How can Pelagius say, "Our power to speak well is from God, but speaking well is our own," when the Lord says that the Spirit of the Father speaks in us? He said, "It is not you who speak," not "It is not you who gave yourselves the power to speak." He said, "It is the Spirit of your Father who speaks in you," not "who gives or gave you the power to speak well" [Matt. 10:20]. Thus he does not indicate the actualization of a capacity; he expresses the accomplishment of cooperation.

How can this proud preacher of free choice say, "Our power to think well is from God, but good thinking is our own"? The humble preacher of grace replies to him, "We are not fit to think anything by ourselves from our own resources. Our competence is from God" [2 Cor. 3:5]. He says, "to think," not "to be able to think."

(XXVI.27) Pelagius therefore should explicitly acknowledge the grace of God which is manifest in the divine discourse. He should not conceal with unblushing insolence the fact that for a long time he denied it. Rather, he should openly confess this with salutary contrition, so that the holy church may rejoice in his true amendment rather than being disturbed by his unyielding obstinacy.

He should distinguish knowledge and love as they ought to be distinguished: knowledge puffs up but charity builds up [1 Cor. 8:1]. Knowledge does not puff up only when charity builds up. Since both of them are God's gifts, though one is greater and the other lesser, he should not praise our justice more than the glory of our Justifier by assigning the lesser of the two to divine assistance and usurping the greater for human decision.

If he agrees that we receive charity by the grace of God, he should not construe this as though any good merits of ours precede it. What good merits could we have had when we did not love God? Before we had love for God we were ourselves loved so that we might receive that love by which we then love. The Apostle John clearly states this, "Not that we had loved God, but because he loved us" [1 John 4:10], and elsewhere, "We love because he has first loved us" [1 John 4:19]. Beautifully expressed and truly said! We would not have love for him unless we had received it from him when he loved us first. Unless we love, what good can we do? Or if we love, how can we fail to do good? Although those who fear but do not love might appear to fulfill God's commands, in the absence of love no work is reckoned good nor is any work properly called good, because "what is not from faith is sin" [Rom. 14:23], and "faith works through love" [Gal. 5:6]. Thus anyone who wants to confess truly the grace of God by which "charity is poured into our hearts through the Holy Spirit who is given to us" [Rom. 5:5] should never doubt that neither true righteousness nor any religious good can be accomplished without this grace. Thus he should not confess it like the one who says, "Grace is given so that what God commands may be more easily accomplished." Here he showed clearly enough that he thinks it can still be done, though not as easily, without grace.

(XXVII.28) Pelagius actually expresses his opinion when, in that treatise addressed to a consecrated virgin to which I have already referred, he says, "We should earn the divine grace and thus with the help of the Holy Spirit we may more easily resist the evil spirit." What reason did he have for interjecting "more easily"? Was the sense of "thus by the help of the Holy Spirit we may resist the evil spirit" incomplete? Or does anyone fail to perceive the damage caused by the addition? He wants us to believe that nature is strong enough to resist the evil spirit in some way, although not as easily, even without the help of the Holy Spirit. By so raising up nature's strength, he actually topples it over.

(XXVIII.29) Again, in the first book of his *On Free Choice*, he says, "Although we have within us free choice, strong and stable for avoiding sin, which the creator has implanted universally in human nature, still in his inestimable goodness he defends us with his daily aid." What need for this aid if free choice is so strong and stable for avoiding sin? Here again, of course, he means that the help is given to make easier through grace what he thinks is accomplished, though not as easily, without grace.

(XXIX.30) Again, in another place in the same book, he says, "So that people may more easily fulfill through grace what they are commanded to do through free choice." Remove the "more easily" and the thought is not only complete but right: "So that people can fulfill through grace what they are commanded to do through free choice." When the "more easily" is included, it insinuates that good works can be accomplished even without God's grace. This opinion is refuted by the one who says, "Without me you can do nothing" [John 15:5].

(XXX.31) Pelagius should correct these assertions lest he fall into something worse. When human weakness has gone astray in the depths of these great questions, and once the truth we have explained becomes manifest so that a person realizes his views were misguided, then a danger arises that diabolical deceitfulness or recklessness will be added to the error, so that the person will either deny he ever held the opinion or defend what he wrongly held. In all the writings of Pelagius and Caelestius which I was able to read, I never found a proper recognition of the grace which justifies us, "by which the love of God is poured into our hearts through the Holy Spirit who is given to us" [Rom. 5:5]. Furthermore, I have never found a proper acknowledgment of the children of the promise of whom the Apostle says, "These children of God are not the children of the flesh but are reckoned children of the promise in the seed" [Rom. 9:8]. When God promises something, we do not achieve it by choice or by nature. He accomplishes it himself through grace.

(32) I will not at this time go into the treatises of Caelestius or the briefs he submitted to church courts. Instead I have had all these sent to you along with other letters I thought necessary. Once you have examined these materials carefully, you can see for yourselves that over and above the natural choice of the will, he finds the grace by which God helps us to avoid evil and do good only in the law and teaching. Thus he asserts that the reason a person must pray is to be shown what he should love and desire.

To put these aside for the moment, Pelagius himself recently sent both letters and a statement of his faith to Rome, addressing Pope Innocent of happy memory, whom he did not know had died. In these letters he explains that there are two charges of which people try to accuse him: one, that he denies the sacrament of baptism to children and promises the kingdom of heaven to some independently of the redemption of Christ; second, that he asserts human power to avoid sin in such a way that he excludes divine aid and places so much confidence in free choice that he disdains the assistance of grace.

This is not the place to detail how his views on the baptism of children pervert Christian faith and Catholic truth, though he does admit that the sacrament should be administered to them. Here, instead, we must pursue what we have already begun, the question of the assistance of grace. Let us then see what response he gives here to the charges he has formulated. To pass over as well his bitter complaints about his enemies, this is what he has to say on the question itself.

(XXXI.33) He says, "This letter will exonerate me before Your Beatitude. In it we say plainly and straightforwardly that we have integral free choice, capable of sinning and not sinning, which is always helped by divine assistance in all its good works." The Lord certainly blessed you with the intelligence to realize that this statement is not adequate to settle the question. We still ask what kind of assistance he would maintain as helping free choice. He might, as usual, mean only the law and teaching. Thus, if you asked why he says "always," he might reply that Scripture says, "I will meditate on his law day and night" [Ps. 1:2].

Once he had made some observations on the human condition and its natural capacity for sinning and not sinning, Pelagius added, "We say that this power of free choice is found universally in all, in Christians, Jews, and Gentiles. By nature free choice is equally in all, but only in Christians is it helped by grace." Again we ask, By what kind of grace? And he could still reply, By the law and Christian doctrine.

(34) No matter what kind of grace he intends, he still says that it is given to these Christians according to merits, even though he had already condemned those who assert this during that famous vindication of his in Palestine, as I have in-

dicated above. These are his exact words, first in referring to non-Christians and then in contrasting them to Christians: "The good of their condition is naked and unprotected in these people, but those who belong to Christ are defended by his aid." In the light of our earlier observations, you will notice that the kind of aid remains unclear. He continues on the subject of non-Christians: "Thus these deserve to be judged and condemned because when they have free choice through which they could come to faith and earn God's grace, they abuse the freedom allowed them. Those who use free choice well merit the Lord's grace, they keep his commandments and deserve to be rewarded." Although he does not clearly specify the nature or quality of the grace, he undeniably asserts that it is given according to merits. When he says that those who use free choice well and thereby merit the Lord's grace should be rewarded, he indicates that it is paid to them as their due.

Where then is the assertion of the Apostle "You are justified by his grace as a gift" [Rom. 3:24]? Where is that "By grace you have been saved" [Eph. 2:8]? Lest they think it by works he adds, "through faith." Again, lest they suppose that faith itself was their own without the grace of God, "and this is not from you; it is the gift of God" [Eph. 2:8]. Thus without any merit we receive the faith that is the beginning of everything else that Pelagius says we receive by merit. If he denies that this is given, what about the text "As God bestowed on each one the measure of faith" [Rom. 12:3]? Or if he admits that it is given but in response to merits rather than bestowed as a gift, what of the text "For Christ's sake you were given not only to believe in him but to suffer for him" [Phil. 1:29]? Paul testifies that the two are given, both that a person believes in Christ and that he suffers for Christ. These people, however, relate faith to free choice in a way that seems to make it an earned rather than a gratuitous grace. On this basis, however, it is no longer a grace, because what is not gratuitous is not grace.

(XXXII.35) Pelagius wants his reader to pass from this letter to the profession of faith that he recounted to you, in which he expounded at great length matters about which no one had questioned him. Let us, however, concentrate on the points actually in contention between us and them. Once he had terminated his disquisition on everything from the unity of the Trinity to the resurrection of the flesh, which no one asked him to present, he said, "And we hold one baptism, which we say should be celebrated for infants in the same sacramental words as for adults" [*Profession of Faith* 7]. Indeed, you say that you heard this from him in person. But what difference does it make for him to say that the sacrament of baptism should be celebrated in the same words for children as for adults? Our concern is with the realities, not the words. I find more significant the report in your letter that he personally responded to your question by saying, "Infants receive baptism for the forgiveness of sins." Here he did not say, "in the words of the forgiveness of sins," but acknowledged that they are baptized for the forgiveness itself. And yet if you had asked him what sin is believed to be forgiven them, he would not have maintained that they have any.

(XXXIII.36) Who would have believed that the opposing opinion was actually hidden beneath this apparently open recognition unless Caelestius had let it out? In his brief that was submitted to the church trial in Rome, he admits that children are baptized for the forgiveness of sins, and then denied that they have original sin.

But let us put aside the baptism of children now and concentrate instead on Pelagius' understanding of the assistance of grace in the profession of faith he sent to Rome. There he says, "We recognize free choice in such a way that we assert that we always need God's help" [*Profession of Faith* 13]. Once again we raise the question of what kind of help he admits we need; again we find his position ambiguous. He could respond that he refers to the law and Christian doctrine which help the natural capacity. We keep searching through their confessions for that grace which the Apostle described,

"God did not give us the spirit of fear, but of strength and charity and continence" [2 Tim. 1:7]. The point is that it does not follow that whoever has the gift of knowledge for learning what he should do also has the gift of charity to do it.

(XXXIV.37) I have read all Pelagius' books and other writings which he mentions in these letters addressed to Pope Innocent of blessed memory, except for the one short letter he says was sent to the holy bishop Constantius. Nowhere have I been able to find a recognition of that grace which not only assists that natural capacity for will and action which he claims we have even if we neither will nor accomplish good, but also, as the support of the Holy Spirit, helps will and action itself.

(XXXV.38) He says, "They should read that letter which we wrote to that holy man, Bishop Paulinus, almost twelve years ago. Its nearly three hundred lines deal almost exclusively with God's grace and help. There we state that without God we can do nothing good." So I read the letter. In practically the whole of it, I found him concerned only with the capability of nature, in which the grace of God almost always consists for him. He restricts Christian grace to such a short space—a mere mention of the name—that his only motive appears to have been a fear of omitting it completely. It never becomes clear, however, whether he means grace as the forgiveness of sins, or also as the teaching of Christ which would include the example of his dealings with people, as he does in some places in his writings, or whether he believes that some assistance for acting well is added to nature and instruction through the inspiration of charity, burning and bright.

(XXXVI.39) He says, "They should also read the letter to the holy bishop Constantius. There in a brief but straightforward way I integrated God's grace and help with human free choice." As I stated above, I have not read this letter. If, however, it is anything like the others he cites, which I do know, neither does it contain what we are seeking.

(XXXVII.40) He says further: "They should read as well the letter he wrote in the East to that consecrated virgin of Christ, Demetrias. There they will find that our praise of human nature always includes the assistance of God's grace." Well, I read it, and although he would seem to be contradicting himself in many other places in his works, this one almost convinced me that he does indeed recognize the grace in question. When, however, some other writings fell into my hands, which he composed later for a broader audience, I understood how even in this letter he could use the term "grace" and conceal his opinions beneath this ambiguous generality. Still, by using the word "grace" he avoids giving offense and disarms opposition. Thus he says in the beginning of this work, "We will labor at this project. We are not discouraged, for we trust that our poor ability is aided by the mother's faith and the virgin's merit." [*To Demetrias* 1.] When he said this, I thought he had acknowledged the grace which helps us to accomplish a task. I did not notice at the time that he could have located this grace in the revelation of doctrine alone.

(41) Elsewhere in the same treatise he says, "If, then, even apart from God, these people demonstrate how God made them, we should recognize what can be accomplished by Christians whose nature has been restored to a better condition by Christ and who are assisted by divine grace" [*To Demetrias* 3]. By the restoration of nature to a better condition, he actually intends the forgiveness of sins. He shows this clearly enough in another place in the same book where he says, "Even those who have been somewhat hardened by a long practice of sinning can be restored through penance" [*To Demetrias* 17]. Here as well, he can locate the help of divine grace in the revelation of doctrine.

(XXXVIII.42) Again, elsewhere in the same letter he says, "If even before the law and long before the coming of our Lord and Savior, some people lived upright and holy lives, as we have said, we should believe all the more that we can do the same after his coming. Christ's grace has restored us and regenerated us as better persons. His blood has purged and cleansed us; his example spurred us to righteousness. We should be better than people who lived before the law." [*To Demetrias* 8.] Notice that he still asserts, although in different words, that the help of grace consists in the forgiveness of sins and the example of Christ. Then he adds, "We should be better than people who lived under the law. As the Apostle says, 'Sin will not rule in you; you are not under the law but under grace' [Rom. 6:14]. Since I think we have adequately explained this, let us now describe a perfect virgin, one who is always illumined by and bears witness to the good of both nature and grace by the holiness of her life." [*To Demetrias* 8–9.] In this statement you should notice that he chose to conclude his remarks in a way which would identify the good of nature with what we receive in being created and that of grace with what we receive in contemplating the example of Christ. Thus he implies that sin was not forgiven for those who were or remain under the law because they either did not have or do not believe the example of Christ.

(XXXIX.43) Other assertions of Pelagius which are to be found not in this treatise but in the third book of *On Free Choice* confirm that this is his view. Addressing his adversary, who has cited the statements of the Apostle "I do not do what I will" [Rom. 7:15] and "I see another law in my body opposing the law of my mind" [Rom. 7:23], and the other things Paul says there, he responds, "You want to apply these statements to the Apostle, but all church writers affirm that they were spoken in the name of a sinner still subject to the law who is held bound by his ingrained customs of vice, like a sort of necessity of sinning. Although he seeks good with his will, his habits drag him headlong into evil. In the person of one individual, he describes the nation that continues to sin under the old law. He says that this people is to be freed from the evil of custom through Christ. Through baptism he first forgives all the sins of those who believe in him. Then he incites them to perfect holiness by imitating him and overcomes their customs of vice by the example of his virtues." Notice how he [Pelagius] explains the helping of those who sin under the law so that they may be justified and liberated through the grace of Christ. Because of their ingrained customs of sinning, the law alone would prove inadequate unless it were supplemented, not by Christ's inspiration of charity through the Holy Spirit, but by his example of virtue which is given to be contemplated and imitated in the teaching of the gospel. In this one place more than in any other, he could have been expected to explain what kind of grace he was talking about. The Apostle concludes the passage to which Pelagius was responding by saying, "Unfortunate person that I am, who will free me from the body of this death? God's grace through our Lord Jesus Christ" [Rom. 7:24, 25]. If Pelagius explains here that this grace consists not in his aid for virtue but in his example for imitation, should we really expect anything stronger from him whenever he uses the term "grace" in a general and ambiguous way?

(XL.44) To go back again to the treatise addressed to the consecrated virgin which we discussed above, we note that he says, "If we submit to God and earn divine grace by doing his will, then with the help of the Holy Spirit we may more easily resist the evil spirit" [*To Demetrias* 25]. In this statement he doubtless intends that we are helped by the grace of the Holy Spirit, not because we cannot resist the tempter by the capacity of nature alone but in order that we may resist more easily. Now whatever the kind or amount of this help, we may assume that for him it consists in the bestowing of knowledge through instruction by the revelation of the Spirit, which we can attain either not at all or only with difficulty through nature.

These, then, are the passages I was able to find in the treatise he addressed to the virgin of Christ where he seems to acknowledge grace. You can certainly see for yourself what they are like.

(XLI.45) Pelagius also says, "Let them read as well the treatise I was forced to publish recently, *On Free Choice*. Then they will realize how unfairly they have slandered us by the charge of denying grace. Throughout nearly the whole text of that work, we acknowledge perfectly and completely both free choice and grace.'' There are four books in this work. I read them; I culled from them the passages I thought should be examined and discussed; and I then dealt with them as I was able before taking up the letters he sent to Rome. Even in these four books, however, his statements about that grace which helps us to avoid evil and do good do not advance in any way beyond the ambiguity of his earlier assertions. He can interpret this ambiguity for his disciples in such a way that they believe in an assistance of grace for the natural capacity which consists only in the law and teaching. Thus they could maintain, as Pelagius expressly asserts in his writings, that prayers are offered only so that teaching may be available to us by divine revelation, not so that a person's mind might be helped to accomplish by love and action what he had learned should be done.

In no way does Pelagius draw back from that most explicit dogma of his in which he establishes the trio of capacity, will, and action, and then says that only the capacity is helped by divine aid, while judging that will and action require no help from God. That assistance which he does grant as an aid to the natural capacity consists in the law and instruction. Even the Holy Spirit, he claims, only reveals this to us, and it is in this context that he concedes that we should pray for it. This assistance of law and instruction was available even in the prophetic period, but the help of grace in the proper sense of the word comes, he thinks, in the example of Christ. You can see, of course, that even this falls within the category of teaching, of that doctrine which is preached to us in the gospel. The result is that once the way in which we should walk has been shown, the strength of free choice makes us self-sufficient and we need no help from anyone else to keep us from failing in the way [Matt. 15:32]. Although he contends that nature alone can even find this way, he concedes that it is easier with the help of grace.

(XLII.46) This, then, is the best I have been able to make

of the references to grace in Pelagius' writings. You realize, of course, that those who hold such views "ignore the justice of God and seek to establish their own" [Rom. 10:3], and that they are far from "what comes to us from God, not from ourselves" [Phil. 3:9], from what they should discover and recognize in the Scriptures, especially those of the holy canon. But they read them according to their own viewpoint and consequently do not perceive the things that are obvious in them. I wish, therefore, that they would at least attend with care to what is proposed on the assistance of divine grace in the writings of Catholic authors whose understanding of the Scriptures they do not question. In this way they might be saved from perishing through their own opinions. Notice the way Pelagius himself praises the holy Ambrose in the third book of his recent treatise, *On Free Choice*, where he cites him in his own defense.

(XLIII.47) Pelagius says, "In the writings of the blessed bishop Ambrose, the Roman faith especially sparkles; he shines as a beautiful blossom among the writers of the Latin church; no enemy has dared disparage his faith and his unblemished understanding of the Scriptures." Notice the high and beautiful praises he heaps upon this man, whose holiness and learning still do not give him an authority comparable to that of the canonical Scriptures. The reason Pelagius so glorifies Ambrose is that he thinks he can use a passage from one of his books to prove that human beings can live without sin. What concerns us immediately, however, is not this question but the assistance of grace which helps us to avoid sinning and to live justly.

(XLIV.48) Pelagius should listen, then, to that venerable bishop teaching in the second book of his *Exposition of the Gospel According to Luke*, where he explains that the Lord also cooperates with our wills. "Certainly you realize that the power of the Lord everywhere cooperates with human efforts No one can build without the Lord; no one can guard without the Lord; no one can begin anything without the Lord [Ps. 127:1]. According to the Apostle, therefore, 'whether you eat or drink, do all to the glory of God' " [1 Cor. 10:31]. [*On Luke* II.84.] You notice how the holy Ambrose rejects even that saying which people often quote, "We begin and God completes," by asserting that no one can even begin anything without God.

Similarly, in the sixth book of the same work, when he is discussing the two debtors of the same creditor, he says, "In human eyes, perhaps, the one who owed more was the greater offender, but the Lord's mercy reversed this so that the one who owed more loves more if he obtains this grace" [*On Luke* VI.25]. Note that this Catholic teacher explicitly asserts that even the love by which a person loves more fully is itself a consequence of the gift of grace.

(XLV.49) Even penance, which is certainly done by the will, is attributed to the efficacy of divine mercy and assistance by the blessed Ambrose in the ninth book of the same work. "The tears which wash away guilt are good. Thus those upon whom Jesus looks weep. Peter denied once and did not weep because the Lord had not looked upon him. He denied a second time and did not weep because the Lord had still not looked upon him. He denied a third time, then Jesus looked upon him, and he wept bitterly" [Luke 22:54–62]. [*On Luke* X.89.] They should read the Gospel and notice that the Lord Jesus was inside at that point, being questioned by the high priests, while the Apostle Peter was outside, down in the courtyard, with the servants sitting by or standing at the fire, as the consistent and accurate narratives of the evangelists make clear [Mark 14:53–72; Matt. 26:57–75; John 18:15–27]. Hence one cannot say that the Lord admonished him in a visible way by looking on him with his bodily eyes. Thus what is written there, "The Lord looked upon him" [Luke 22:61], was done within, in the mind, in the will. The Lord came to his rescue secretly; he touched his heart; he recalled his memory; by his grace he entered the depths of Peter's being; he moved his inner feelings and led them forth into outer tears. Notice how in his assistance God is present to our choices and actions. Notice how "he works in us both to will and to work" [Phil. 2:13].

(50) Similarly, the same holy Ambrose in the same book says, "Now if Peter said, 'Even if others are scandalized, I will not be scandalized' [Matt. 26:33], and then fell, who else has a right to presume on himself? Similarly, because David had said, 'I said in my abundance, I shall not be moved forever' [Ps. 30:6], he confessed that his boasting worked against him, 'You turned your face away and I was shaken' " [Ps. 30:7]. [*On Luke* X.91.] Pelagius should heed this great man's teaching and imitate his believing, since he praised his faith and doctrine. He should humbly hear him and faithfully imitate him. He should not presumptuously trust in himself lest he perish. Why does this sailor want to go down in that sea from which Peter was rescued by the Rock?

(XLVI.51) Pelagius should hear this same bishop of God speaking in the sixth book of the same work: "The evangelist himself explains why they did not receive him, 'Because his face was set toward Jerusalem' [Luke 9:53]. His disciples were determined that he be welcomed into Samaria. But God calls whom he chooses and makes whom he wills religious." [*On Luke* VII.27.] What insight of a man of God, drawn right from the fountain of God's grace! "God," he says, "calls whom he chooses and makes whom he wills religious." This is what the prophet declared, "I will have mercy on whom I shall have had mercy, and I will show mercy to whom I shall have been merciful" [Exod. 33:19; Rom. 9:15]. This is what the Apostle asserts, "Thus it is not from the person willing or striving but from God having mercy" [Rom. 9:16]. This, then, is what God's spokesman in our own times says, "He calls whom he chooses and makes whom he wills religious." Will anyone dare to say that a person is not already religious 'who runs to the Lord, seeks to be guided by him, joins his own will to his will, and who by adhering to him becomes one spirit with him, according to the Apostle" [1 Cor. 6:17]? But Pelagius asserts that this great work of such a religious person "is accomplished by free choice alone." The blessed Ambrose, whom he praised so highly with his own mouth, opposes him in saying, "The Lord calls whom he chooses and makes whom he wills religious." God makes whom he wills religious, therefore, so that he will run to the Lord, seek to be ruled by him, join his own will to his will, and by adhering to him become one spirit with him according to the Apostle [1 Cor. 6:17]. All this is done only by a religious person. Hence, who will do it unless God makes him do it?

(XLVII.52) In discussing this question of the will's choice and God's grace, the proper distinctions are always difficult to make. When you defend free choice, you seem to be denying God's grace; then when you affirm God's grace, people think you are excluding free choice. Thus Pelagius can take refuge in the windings of this complexity. He could profess his agreement with all the statements we have cited from the holy Ambrose, could protest that he holds these doctrines and has always held them, and he could then attempt to explain each point in a way that would make it even support his position. In this matter of divine grace and help, therefore, I must ask you to bear in mind the three elements he has clearly distinguished: to be able, to will, and to do, that is, capacity, will, and action. I will cast the question in these his own terms. Let him agree with us that God not only helps the capacity even if a person neither wills nor acts well, but also helps willing and action itself, so that a person wills and works well. Unlike the capacity, these two are in a person only when he actually wills and acts well. Let him agree, further, that without this help we neither choose nor accomplish anything good. Let him admit that this is the grace of God in our Lord Jesus Christ, through which he makes us righteous by his justice rather than our own, that our justice is that which comes from him. If he agrees to these propositions, I see no further reason for dispute between us on this question of the grace of God.

(XLVIII.53) Pelagius' reason for honoring the holy Ambrose so highly is a passage he found in his writings where in praising Zechariah and Elizabeth he says that a person can be without sin in this life. This could happen if God willed it, of course, since God can do all things. He should notice, however, in what sense it was said. The reference, so far as I can tell, was to upright and praiseworthy dealings with other people. In these, no fair person could accuse or find fault with them. Zechariah and his wife are called upright and blameless before God because other people were not deceived in this estimation of them [Luke 1:6]; they actually were in the eyes of God exactly as they appeared to others. The reference is not to that fullness of righteousness in which we will live truly and completely, spotless and perfect. [*On Luke* I.15–21.] Thus even the Apostle Paul said he was "blameless according to that justice which is from the law" [Phil. 3:6]. Zechariah also lived without blame according to the law. But the Apostle considered this righteousness as dung and trash in comparison to that justice for which we hope [Phil. 3:8] and for which we should now hunger and thirst so that we may some day be filled in reality [Matt. 5:6] with what is now ours in faith as long as "the just lives by faith" [Rom. 1:17].

(XLIX.54) Pelagius should listen to this venerable bishop, then, when in expounding the prophet Isaiah he says that no one can be without sin in this world. No one can claim that when Ambrose says "in this world" he means "in loving this world," since he is talking about the Apostle who said, "Our citizenship (*conversatio*) is in heaven" [Phil. 3:20]. The bishop explains the meaning of this: "The Apostle says that there are many who are perfect with him while in this world. They could not have been perfect, however, if the standard were true perfection. Because he himself said, 'Now we see darkly through a mirror, but then we shall see face to face. Now I know partially, but then I shall know fully just as I am known' [1 Cor. 13:12]. Thus there are the unblemished in this world and there will be the unblemished in the kingdom of God. But if you are more exacting, it is certain that no one can be spotless, because no one is without sin" [Ambrose, *On Isaiah*, fragment 5]. Thus the passage of the holy Ambrose which Pelagius uses to support this position may have been written within a certain perspective, on some assumption which he did not fully investigate; if not, if that holy and humble man did judge that Zechariah and Elizabeth had that full and perfect justice to which nothing can be added, Ambrose undeniably corrected his opinion after considering the matter more carefully.

(L.55) Pelagius should notice that in the very place from which he took the passage of Ambrose which he liked, it is also said that "it is impossible for human nature to be unblemished from the beginning" [*On Luke* I.17]. Here indeed the venerable Ambrose testifies to the weakness and infirmity of that natural capacity which Pelagius refuses to regard as corrupted by sin and which he therefore praises extravagantly. Ambrose undeniably contradicts Pelagius' intention, but not the Apostolic truth, where we read, "Even we were once by nature children of wrath just like the rest" [Eph. 2:3]. This nature is the one corrupted and condemned through the sin of the first man which came from his free choice. Only the divine grace comes to its aid through the mediator of God and humanity, the Almighty Physician.

We have spent enough time discussing God's help for our justification, by which he cooperates in all good with those who love him [Rom. 8:28], whom he himself has loved first and given to love him [1 John 4:19]. Let us take up now, as far as God will help us, that sin which along with death through one person "entered the world and so has spread to everyone" [Rom. 5:12]. We shall explain what seems necessary against those who have openly sallied forth into the error opposed to this truth.

ON REBUKE AND GRACE

(X.26) Another question arises here which should not be ignored. With the help of the Lord, who holds both ourselves and our words in his hand [Wisd. of Sol. 7:16], we should discuss and resolve it. In reference to God's gift of perseverance in good until the end of life, we are asked our opinion about the first human being, who was certainly created upright and free of fault. I do not pose the question "How could someone who lacked so necessary a divine gift as perseverance have been without fault?" This question is easily resolved by noting that he lacked perseverance precisely because he did not remain in that good which he originally had without fault. He began to have a fault from the moment he fell. Since it started then, he was clearly blameless before the defect began. To be without fault is one thing; to remain in that goodness which is without fault is quite another. By the very fact that we do not say he was never without fault, but say instead that he did not continue without fault, we clearly indicate that originally he had been without fault and blame him for not remaining in that good condition.

What requires fuller discussion and more careful investigation, however, is the question posed by those who say, "If he had perseverance in that rectitude in which he was created without fault, he certainly persevered in it. If he persevered, he certainly did not sin and did not abandon God and his own rectitude. Truth, however, asserts that he did sin and deserted the good. Hence he did not have perseverance in that good; and if he did not have it, he did not receive it. How could he have received perseverance and then not have persevered? Further, if he did not have it because he did not receive it, then how did he sin in not persevering when he did not receive perseverance? You cannot reply that he had not received it because he was not separated out from that lump of condemnation by the abundance of grace. That mass of perdition did not exist in the human race before this one from whom we derive our corrupted beginning had himself sinned."

(27) Therefore we properly believe and confess to our salvation that the God and Lord of all, who created all things exceedingly good, both foreknew that evils would arise from these goods and knew that it was more appropriate for his sovereign goodness to deal well with these evils than to pre-

vent their occurrence. He so arranged the life of angels and humans that he showed first what their free choice could achieve and then what the favor of his grace and the judgment of his justice could accomplish. Through free choice some of the angels, whose chief is called the devil, became fugitives from the Lord God. When they took to flight from his goodness in which they had been happy, however, they could not escape his judgment through which they became miserable. Through free choice the other angels stood firm in truth and thereby merited the certainty of knowing that they would never fail. From the fact that the Scriptures tell us that none of the holy angels will fail, we can conclude that they must know this more fully themselves, since this truth is revealed to them in a higher way. We are promised life without end and equality with the angels [Matt. 22:30]. By this promise we are certain that once we have entered life after the judgment we will never fall from it. Now if the angels do not know the same thing about themselves, we will be happier than they, not their equals. Truth, however, has promised us equality with them. It is certain, therefore, that they know by vision what we know by faith: that none of the holy angels will ever fall.

The devil and his angels were happy before they failed and did not know they would fall into misery. They would have received a fuller happiness, however, if they had stood fast in truth through free choice. As a reward for their endurance they would have received that fullness of the highest happiness which consists in such a great abundance of love of God through the Holy Spirit that they could no longer fall and would know this with certainty. They did not have this complete happiness. Still, since they did not know they were going to be miserable, they enjoyed a real, though lesser, happiness without defect. For if they had already known of their coming failure and eternal punishment, they could not have been happy. Apprehension of such evil would have made them miserable even then.

(28) Thus God created humanity with free choice. Al-

though he did not know about his future fall, Adam was happy because he realized that he had the power to avoid both death and misery. If by free choice he had willed to remain in this upright and faultless condition, then as reward for this endurance and without ever experiencing death or misfortune, he would have received the same fullness of happiness which the angels enjoy: to be unable to fall later and to know this with certitude. He could not have been happy in paradise—indeed, he would not have been in paradise, since no one should be unhappy there—if foreknowledge of his fall had made him miserable with fear of such an evil. Because he abandoned God through free choice, however, he experienced God's just judgment. He was condemned along with his whole race, which was still wholly contained within him and thus sinned with him. God's grace liberates some of this race and frees them from that condemnation which now holds them bound. Thus even if none were set free, no one could justly complain about God's judgment. A large number are actually liberated, though they are only a few in comparison with those who perish. Grace does this, gratuitously, and it deserves gratitude. Thus no one should think it comes from his merits and be puffed up; but every mouth should be shut; and whoever boasts should boast in the Lord [Rom. 3:19; 1 Cor. 1:31].

(XI.29) What then? Was Adam deprived of God's grace? He had a great grace, but it was a different kind. He was surrounded by the good things he had received from his creator, goods which he had not matched by his merits, and he suffered no evil. In contrast, the saints in this life, who are the objects of this liberating grace, are surrounded by evils; from these they cry to God, "Deliver us from evil" [Matt. 6:13]. Amid those goods, he did not need the death of Christ; but they are absolved from hereditary and personal guilt by the blood of the Lamb. He did not need the help they implore when they say, "I see another law in my members opposing the law of my mind and leading me captive to the law of sin in my body. Unfortunate person that I am, who will deliver me from the body of this death? God's grace through Jesus Christ our Lord'' [Rom. 7:23–25]. In danger and struggling in this battle in which the flesh lusts against the spirit and the spirit against the flesh within them, the saints plead that strength to fight and win be given them through the grace of Christ. Adam was neither tried nor troubled by such strife and division of self against self; in that place of happiness he enjoyed peace with himself.

(30) Although for the present it may not be a more joyful grace, the saints do need a stronger grace. What grace could be stronger than the only-begotten Son of God, co-eternal and equal to the Father, made human for them and then without either hereditary or personal sin crucified by human sinners. Although he rose on the third day never to die again, he endured death for the sake of mortals and restored life to the dead. Thus, redeemed by his blood and receiving so great and precious a gift, the saints can say, "If God is for us, who is against us? He did not spare his own Son but delivered him over for all of us. Will he not give us all things with him?'' [Rom. 8:31–32]. In an assumption at once uniquely wonderful and wonderfully unique, God took up our nature, the flesh and rational soul of the human Christ, so that without any preceding merits of his own justice, this human being began to be the Son of God, so that from the beginning of his own existence he was one person with the Word who is without beginning. Nor is anyone so blindly ignorant of this event and of the faith that he would dare to assert that although the Son of Man was born of the Holy Spirit and the Virgin Mary, he earned the rank of being Son of God through free choice by living well and doing good works without sinning. The Gospel refutes this by saying, "The Word was made flesh'' [John 1:14]. Where was this done except in the womb of the Virgin, the place where the human Christ began? Further, when the Virgin asked how what had been announced to her would happen, the angels responded, "The Holy Spirit will come over you and the power of the Most High will overshadow you. Therefore, the holy one to be born of you will be

called the Son of God'' [Luke 1:35]. He did not say ''therefore'' because of good works, which the unborn child had
not yet·done. He said it because ''the Holy Spirit will come
over you and the power of the Most High will overshadow
you, the holy one to be born of you will be called the Son of
God.'' This birth, which joined the human to God and the
flesh to the Word in the unity of one person, was undeniably
gratuitous. Good works followed; they did not earn this
birth. Nor was there reason to fear that once human nature
had been assumed by God the Word into this indescribable union it might then sin by free choice of the will. The
assumption itself was such that the human nature taken by
God would allow no evil impulse of the will to enter it.
Through this Mediator, whom he took up in such a way that
he would never be evil or even be changed from having been
evil to being always good, God shows that when he redeems
by Christ's blood, he himself converts people from evil and
makes them eternally good.

(31) The first human being did not have this grace which
would make him never choose evil. If he had willed to
persevere in the grace he did have, however, he would never
have been evil. Without this grace, he could not have been
good even by free choice, though by free choice he could
abandon the grace. Nor did God intend him to be deprived
of his grace, which he left to his free choice. Free choice is
adequate for evil, but it can manage good only if it is helped
by Sovereign Good. If this person had not abandoned that
assistance by free choice, he would always have been good.
He deserted, however, and was deserted in turn. The help
was not the kind that would cause him to will; he could remain in it or abandon it by choosing. This, then, is the first
grace given to the First Adam. A stronger grace is in the Second Adam. By the first grace, a person has justice if he wills
it. The second grace can do more; it moves a person to will,
indeed, to will so strongly and love so ardently that by the opposing will of the spirit he conquers the lusting will of the
flesh. The first grace, which showed the power of free choice,

was not insignificant: without this assistance a person could not persevere in good, although he could abandon the help if he so chose. The second grace is greater because a grace which restores a person's lost liberty and enables him to attain and remain in good if he so wills does not do enough unless it also causes him to will it.

(32) God had given Adam good will, then, had created him in it by making him upright. God had also given the help necessary to persevere in good if Adam so willed. The willing itself, however, he left to his free choice. Adam could have persevered if he willed, because he had the help through which he could and without which he could not steadfastly retain the good he willed. Thus the blame is his because he refused to persevere, just as the merit would have been his if he had chosen to persevere. The holy angels did persevere. When the others fell by free choice, they stood fast through the same free choice and earned the reward due for this perseverance. They received that fullness of happiness which makes them absolutely certain that they will always have it. Since angels and humans were created in a nature which made them unable to be constant without divine aid, unless they were given this assistance when they were first created, they would not have been culpable if they had fallen. They would not have had the help without which they could not stand. Now, however, people are already being punished for sin when they do not receive such help; and the help which is given to others is by grace, not according to merit. We whom God is pleased to aid more fully through Jesus Christ our Lord receive not only the assistance necessary to be able to persevere if we so will, but the kind of help which also makes us will it. This grace of God not only makes us able to do what we will in receiving and steadfastly retaining good, but it actually makes us will to do what we can. This was not the situation of the first human being: he had the first of these but not the second. He did not need grace to receive good because he had not yet lost it. He did need the help of grace, however to persevere in good and simply could not persevere

without it. He had received the capacity to persevere if he chose, but he did not have the will to do what he could. Had he had it, he would have persevered; he could have persevered if he so willed. His refusal to do so came from his free choice which at that point had the freedom to will either well or ill. Freedom will be greater once free choice is unable to serve sin. Human beings were to have attained this, just as the angels received it, as an earned reward. Now, however, good merit has been lost by sin, and what was to be a reward for merit has become a gift of grace to those who are liberated.

(XII.33) We must examine carefully and specify exactly the difference between these pairs: to be able not to sin and not to be able to sin; to be able not to die and not to be able to die; to be able not to abandon the good and not to be able to abandon the good. The first human being was able not to sin, not to die, not to desert the good. We certainly could not say that someone with his type of freedom of choice was not able to sin. Or that someone who was told, "If you sin, you will die the death" [Gen. 2:17], was not able to die. Or that he was not able to abandon the good, when he actually deserted it by sinning and then died. Thus the original freedom of will was to be able not to sin; the final freedom will be much greater—not to be able to sin. The original immortality was to be able not to die; the final will be greater—not to be able to die. The original power of perseverance was to be able not to abandon the good; the final will be the blessedness of perseverance itself—not to be able to desert the good. Nor should we infer that the original goods were either insignificant or not really good, because the final ones will be better and stronger.

(34) The forms of assistance must be similarly distinguished. The help without which something is not done is one thing; the help by which it is actually accomplished is another. Without food we cannot live, but the availability of food does not cause those who prefer to die to continue living. Thus the assistance of food is necessary for us to live, but

does not itself effect our living. When happiness is given to someone who did not have it, however, he immediately becomes happy. It is not only a necessary help but one which actually accomplishes its purpose. Thus it is a help both by which something happens and without which it does not happen. If a person receives happiness, he immediately becomes happy; but if he never receives it, he never will be. A person does not live simply as a consequence of having food, though he cannot live without it.

The first human being, then, had been created upright and had thereby received the ability not to sin, not to die, and not to desert this good. The assistance which he received for perseverance did not actually accomplish his perseverance, though without it he would have been unable to persevere through free choice. The saints who are predestined now for the kingdom of God do not receive this kind of assistance. The actual persevering is given to them so that they are not only unable to persevere without this gift, but through it do not fail to persevere. Christ said not only, "Without me you can do nothing" [John 15:5], but also, "You have not chosen me, but I have chosen you and appointed you that you should go and bear fruit and that your fruit should endure" [John 15:16]. By this statement he indicated that he had given them not only justice but perseverance in it as well. When Christ appoints them to go and bear fruit and that their fruit endure, will anyone dare to assert that it will not, or even that it might not endure? "God's call and gifts are irrevocable" [Rom. 11:29], and they were called according to his purpose. With Christ praying for them that their faith not fail, it certainly will not fail before the end. Thus they will endure faithfully unto the end, and the end of this life will not find them any other way.

(35) A greater liberty is necessary to withstand these many and great trials which were not encountered in paradise, a freedom fortified and strengthened by the gift of perseverance so that it conquers this world with all its desires, all its terrors, all its errors. The martyrdoms of the saints taught

this. Adam had no one menacing him and had the command of a threatening God; yet he exercised his free choice and did not remain in such blessedness when it was so easy to avoid sin. In contrast, the martyrs had the world not simply threatening, but raging against them; yet they stood firm in the faith. He saw before him the goods he would lose; they did not see the future goods they would receive. Whence the difference in the outcome, then, except from the one whose mercy they received to be faithful [1 Cor. 7:25], from whom they received not a spirit of fear to give in to their persecutors but a Spirit of strength and charity and continence to overcome all threats, all enticements, all tortures [2 Tim. 1:7]? In being created he received free will without any sin and then enslaved it to sin. But when their wills were slaves of sin, they were freed through him who said, "If the Son frees you, you will be free indeed" [John 8:36]. Through grace they receive such freedom that although they struggle against sinful desires as long as they live and are caught unawares by some of them so that they pray daily, "Forgive us our debts" [Matt. 6:12], still they no longer give in to that sin which is unto death, that sin to which the Apostle John refers: "There is a sin unto death; and I do not say that you should pray for it" [1 John 5:16]. Because he did not specify this sin, many different interpretations can be given of it. I myself think that this sin is to abandon the faith which works through love even unto death. In no longer serving this sin, the saints do not have the freedom in which Adam was originally created; rather, they are freed by God's grace through the Second Adam. Through this liberation they have a freedom of choice in which they actually serve God and are not taken captive by the devil. They are liberated from sin, become servants of justice, and stand firm in it to the end. God gives them this perseverance. He foreknew and predestined them, called them according to his purpose, justified and glorified them [Rom. 8:28–30]. He has already accomplished even the future things which he promised for them. "Abraham believed in his promise, and this was reckoned to him as righteous ness" [Rom. 4:3]. "He glorified God, fully believing, as the Scripture says, that he has power to do what he promised" [Rom. 4:20-21].

(36) Thus God makes them good so that they might then do good. He did not promise these heirs to Abraham because he foreknew that they would make themselves good. In that case, what he promised would have been theirs, not his own. But this is not what Abraham believed, for "he was not weak in faith but glorified God, fully believing that he could do what he promised" [Rom. 4:20-21]. It does not say "that he could promise what he foreknew" or "that he could present what he predicted" or even "that he could foreknow what he promised," but rather, "that he could do what he promised." Thus he makes them good and also makes them persevere in that good. Those who fall and perish, however, were not counted among the predestined. The Apostle says of all the reborn who are living devoutly, "Who are you to judge another's servant? He stands or falls by his own master's judgment" [Rom. 14:4]. Immediately, however, he focused on the predestined and said, "But he will stand." To prevent anyone from claiming this for himself, he added, "God has the power to make him stand" [Rom. 14:4]. Perseverance is given by God, who has the power to stabilize those who are standing so that they stand with perseverance or to restore those who have fallen: "The Lord lifts up the crushed" [Ps. 146:8].

(37) The will of the first human being had such power that he was not given God's gift of perseverance but allowed to decide for himself whether or not to persevere. His will was created without any sin; and none of his other desires opposed his will, so that the choice of persevering in such goodness and such aptitude for good living was appropriately committed to him. Indeed, God foreknew what he would unjustly do; but he only foreknew and did not determine him to do it. At the same time he knew what he would justly do about him.

Now, however, once humanity has deserved to lose that

great liberty by sinning, it has a weakness which must be assisted by even greater gifts. God was pleased to suppress completely the pride of human presumption so that no flesh, no human being, might boast in his presence [1 Cor. 1:29]. What would flesh boast of except its merits? It could have had these merits, but it lost the opportunity. Moreover, it lost the free choice through which merit could be acquired; the only freedom now remaining comes from liberating grace. No flesh, therefore, may boast in God's presence. The unjust have no reason at all to glorify themselves. The just have their merits only from God, and no glory besides him whom they praise: "You are my glory; you lift up my head" [Ps. 3:3]. Thus the scriptural text "No flesh may boast in his presence" [1 Cor. 1:29] applies to every human being, while the text "One who boasts should boast in the Lord" [1 Cor. 1:31] applies to the just. The Apostle shows this quite clearly. Once he had said, "So that no flesh may boast in his presence," to prevent the saints thinking they still had no glory at all, he added, "Through him you are in Jesus Christ, whom God made our wisdom, our justice, holiness, and redemption, so that one who boasts should boast in the Lord" [1 Cor. 1:30–31]. This is why in this valley of tears, where human life upon earth is a trial, "power is perfected in weakness" [2 Cor. 12:9]. What power is this except that "anyone who boasts should boast in the Lord"?

(38) Thus even for their perseverance in good, God wants the saints to boast in him rather than in their own strength. He not only gives them the help he gave Adam, which is necessary for them to persevere if they so choose; he also works the willing itself in them. Since they will not actually persevere unless they both can and will, in the abundance of his grace he gives them both the capacity and the will to persevere. Their wills are so inflamed by the Holy Spirit that they are able because they so will, and they so will because God causes them to will. Strength should be perfected in the weakness of this life to check the soaring of pride. If God left the decision to them in the midst of such weakness, so that he

gave them only that help which is necessary for them to persevere if they choose and did not also cause the willing itself
in them, then their will would fail by its own weakness in the
face of such great and numerous temptations. They would be
unable to persevere because in their weakness they would fail
to will it; or their weak wills would not choose it so firmly that
they would be able to do it.

Thus the weakness of the human will is assisted so that
under the influence of divine grace it moves unfailingly and
unconquerably. Although weak, it does not fail; nor is it
overcome by any opposition. Through the strength of God a
sick and feeble human will perseveres in a good which is still
small, while the strong and healthy will of the first human
being did not persevere in a much fuller good. Adam had the
strength of free choice and he would have had the assistance
necessary to persevere if he had so chosen, but he did not
have the assistance by which God would actually cause his
willing. God set the strong one free and permitted him to do
what he chose; he guards the weak so that by his gift the
saints unfailingly choose the good and unfailingly refuse to
abandon it.

Thus we understand Christ's statement "I have prayed for
you that your faith may not fail" [Luke 22:32] as addressed to
those built on the rock. Thus the person belonging to God
"should boast in the Lord," not only because he received
mercy to be faithful, but also because this faith does not fail.

VII.

The Synod of Orange, A.D. 529

*Preface of Caesarius of Arles added to
the acts of the council and
their pontifical confirmation*

This volume contains the Synod of Orange, which was con-
firmed by the decree of the holy Pope Boniface. Anyone,
therefore, whose belief about grace and free choice differs
from what is stated by this decree or established by this synod
must realize that he opposes the Apostolic See and the
Church Universal throughout the whole world. This volume
also contains statements of the holy ancient fathers. Although
the Synod of Orange preceded the decree, it seemed proper
to me that, out of reverence for the Apostolic See, the decree
of the Lord Pope should appear first.

LETTER OF POPE BONIFACE II TO CAESARIUS

Boniface to his dear brother Caesarius:

(1) We have received the letters Your Fraternity sent to us
through our son the presbyter and abbot Arminius. In that
love which joins us together in God, you apparently wrote
without knowing about the priesthood which has been com
mitted to me. In these letters you thought you were asking
me to intervene to facilitate what you were seeking from Pope
Felix, our predecessor of happy memory, for the strengthening of the Catholic faith. Since, however, the heavenly will
had so disposed that what you had hoped from him you actually asked of us, we did not delay to give a Catholic re-

sponse to this petition which you conceived in commendable concern for the faith.

You indicate that some bishops of Gaul, even though they agree that other good things come from God's grace, want the faith by which we believe in Christ to be from nature rather than from grace. They impiously assert that it remained in the power of human free choice which comes from Adam and is not now bestowed on individuals by the abundance of divine mercy. For the sake of dispelling this confusion, you ask us to confirm with the authority of the Apostolic See your declaration in which, on the contrary and according to Catholic truth, you define that true faith in Christ and the beginning of every good intention is inspired in the mind of each person through the intervention of God's grace.

(2) Many of the fathers, the chief being Bishop Augustine of happy memory, as well as our predecessor bishops of the Apostolic See, are known to have given this matter the fullest consideration. Thus no one should any longer remain uncertain that faith itself comes to us from grace. We have decided therefore to refrain from an elaborate response, especially since, according to the statements you selected from the Apostle, "I have received mercy to be faithful" [1 Cor. 7:25] and elsewhere, "For Christ's sake you were given not only to believe in him but also to suffer for him" [Phil. 1:29], it is obvious that the faith by which we believe in Christ, as indeed every good thing, comes to individual persons from the gift of heavenly grace.

We rejoice that Your Fraternity judged according to Catholic faith in the conference held with other priests of Gaul. On these questions they defined with one accord, as you indicate, that the faith by which we believe in Christ is bestowed by the intervention of divine grace, adding especially that without God's grace no one can will, begin, perform, or accomplish anything good in God's sight. Thus the Savior says, "Without me you can do nothing" [John 15:5]. This is both Catholic and certain, because in all good things, of which faith is tne chief, the divine mercy intervenes on our behalf while we are still refusing in order to make us willing; it is upon us when we will; and it follows us so that we will continue in faith. Thus the prophet David says, "My God will go before me with his mercy" [Ps. 59:10] and also "My mercy is with him" [Ps. 89:24] and elsewhere "His mercy follows me" [Ps. 23:6]. Similarly, the blessed Paul says, "Who has first given to him so that he might be repaid? For from him and through him and in him are all things" [Rom. 11:35–36]. We are amazed that those who think the contrary are so weighed down with the relics of ancient error that they believe they come to Christ not by the kindness of God but by the goodness of nature; that they say that the goodness of nature itself, which everyone knows was corrupted by Adam's sin, is actually more the cause of our faith than Christ himself. We wonder why they do not realize that they are protesting against the Lord's statement "No one comes to me unless it is given to him by my Father" [John 6:65] and that they oppose what the blessed Paul proclaimed to the Hebrews: "Let us rush into the struggle proposed to us, looking to the founder and the fulfillment of faith, Jesus Christ" [Heb. 12:1–2]. Given all this, we cannot discover what capacity they attribute to the human will for believing in Christ without God's grace, since Christ himself is the founder and fulfillment of faith. Therefore, we received your confession with similar sentiments, and we approve it as written above [below] as in accord with the Catholic standards of the fathers.

(3) On the basis of their own profession, we can press the argument against those who want to attribute to grace all the other good things which come in second place after faith has preceded. All the more should they be forced to ascribe faith to the gift of grace, because without faith no one can perform anything good in God's sight, as the blessed Apostle says, "Everything that is not from faith is sin" [Rom. 14:23]. Given this, either they will attribute no good to grace if they determine to remove faith from it; or, if they say that any good is from grace, they must necessarily ascribe faith itself to grace. For if without faith there is no good and they deny that

faith itself comes from grace, then no good should be attributed to grace—which is unacceptable. Every good is clearly a
divine gift, as it is written, "Every good gift, every perfect gift
is from above, descending from the Father of lights" [James
1:17]. They admit, as you say, that the other gifts are given
through grace, and they do not doubt that all these good
things are upheld by faith. Faith, therefore, must necessarily
be attributed to grace, since the good things which they do
attribute to grace are inseparable from it.

(4) Having briefly noted these points, we decided against
responding to the remaining absurdities of the Pelagian error
apparently contained in that letter which you say was sent to
you by a certain priest. We hope that through the ministry
and teaching of Your Fraternity the divine mercy will deign
to work in the hearts of all the dissenters you report, so that
once they realize that they are ready to defend what they had
persistently worked to attack, they will believe that every
good will comes from divine grace, not from themselves. For
it is written, "The will is prepared by the Lord" [Prov. 8:35
in LXX] and elsewhere: "I know that I could not be continent
unless God had given this; and it was wisdom to know whose
gift it was" [Wisd. of Sol. 8:21].

May God keep you safe, dear brother.

*Given on the eighth day before the Calends of February, in
the year of consulate of the honorable Lampadius and Orestes
[25 January 531].*

CANONS OF ORANGE

By the mercy of God, at the invitation of Liberius we had
gathered together to dedicate the basilica which this most
honorable prefect, our noble son, had with faithful devotion
constructed in the city of Orange. A spiritual conference took
place among us on matters regarding the faith of the church.
We realized then that there are some who, through simplicity
and without thinking, wish to hold opinions on grace and
free choice which are not in accord with the rule of the Cath-

olic faith. Thus it seemed reasonable and right to us, in accord with the advice and authority of the Apostolic See, that we should instruct these people who are not thinking as they should by publishing for everyone's observance and undersigning with our own hands a few articles sent to us by the Apostolic See that had been gathered from the books of the Holy Scriptures by the ancient fathers on this particular question. Once he has read these articles, anyone who up until now has not believed as he ought about grace and free choice should not hesitate to direct his mind to those things which are proper to the Catholic faith.

(1) If anyone says that the whole person, that is, in both body and soul, was not changed for the worse through the offense of Adam's transgression, but that only the body became subject to corruption with the liberty of the soul remaining unharmed, then he has been deceived by Pelagius' error and opposes the Scripture which says, "The soul which sins shall die" [Ezek. 18:20] and "Do you not know that if you show yourselves ready to obey anyone, you are the slaves of the one you obey?" [Rom. 6:16] and "A person is judged the slave of the one who conquers him" [2 Pet. 2:19].

(2) If anyone asserts that the transgression of Adam harmed him alone and not his progeny, or that the damage is only by the death of the body which is a punishment for sin, and thus does not confess that the sin itself which is the death of the soul also passed through one person into the whole human race, then he does injustice to God, contradicting the Apostle who says, "Through one person sin entered the world and through sin death, and thus it passed to all humans, in whom all have sinned" [Rom. 5:12].

(3) If anyone says that God's grace can be acquired by human appeals but not that grace itself makes us appeal, he contradicts the prophet Isaiah or the Apostle who says the same thing, "I was found by those who did not seek me; I showed myself plainly to those who did not ask for me" [Isa. 65:1; Rom. 10:20].

(4) If anyone contends that God waits for our decision to

cleanse us from sin and does not confess that the bestowal of the Spirit and his action in us moves us to will to be cleansed, he opposes this Holy Spirit who says through Solomon, "The will is prepared by the Lord" [Prov. 8:35 in LXX], and the salutary preaching of the Apostle, "It is God who works in you both to will and to accomplish for good will" [Phil. 2:13].

(5) If anyone says that, like its growth, the beginning of faith and the willingness to trust by which we believe in him who justifies the ungodly and attain the regeneration of holy baptism is present in us naturally and not through the gift of grace, that is, through the inspiration of the Holy Spirit who corrects our will from its infidelity to faith, from ungodliness to piety, then he is convicted by the statement of the blessed Paul of opposing the Apostolic teaching "We trust that the one who began this good work in you will complete it on the day of Christ Jesus" [Phil. 1:6] and also: "For the sake of Christ you were given not only to believe in him, but also to suffer for him" [Phil. 1:29] and "You were saved by grace through faith, and this is not from you but is God's gift" [Eph. 2:8]. Anyone who says that the faith by which we believe in God is natural also asserts that all those who are strangers to the church of Christ are also faithful in some way.

(6) If anyone says that mercy is divinely bestowed on us when without God's grace we believe, will, desire, try, labor, pray, watch, apply ourselves, ask, seek, and knock, but does not confess that the bestowal and inspiration of the Holy Spirit brings us the strength to believe, to will, or to do all these things as we ought; and if he thus subordinates the help of grace to either human humility or obedience, and does not admit that our being humble and obedient is itself a gift of grace, then he opposes the Apostle who says, "What do you have that you have not received?" [1 Cor. 4:7] and "By the grace of God I am what I am" [1 Cor. 15:10].

(7) If anyone affirms that any good which belongs to the salvation of eternal life can be thought of or chosen in a profitable way, or that consent can be given to the salvific, the

evangelical preaching through the strength of nature without the illumination and inspiration of the Holy Spirit who gives everyone delight in consenting to the truth, then he is deceived by an heretical spirit and does not understand God's voice speaking in the Gospel, "Without me you can do nothing" [John 15:5] and the statement of the Apostle "We are not capable of thinking anything by ourselves from our own resources; our adequacy is from God" [2 Cor. 3:5].

(8) If anyone maintains that some come to the grace of baptism by mercy but others can attain it through free choice which stands vitiated in everyone born of the transgression of the first human being, he is shown to be a stranger to the true faith. In saying this, he either asserts that not everyone's free choice is weakened through the first person's sin, or he obviously thinks it is wounded. but only in a way that still allows them the strength to search out the mystery of eternal salvation by themselves without God's revelation. The Lord himself showed how false this is in testifying that not certain ones, but no one at all, could come to him unless the Father had drawn him [John 6:44]. Thus he said to Peter, "Blessed are you, Simon, son of John, because flesh and blood did not reveal this to you but my Father who is in heaven" [Matt. 16:17]. Similarly the Apostle says, "No one can proclaim Jesus Lord except in the Holy Spirit" [1 Cor. 12:3].

(9) The help of God. It is God's gift for us to think properly and to restrain our feet from falsehood and injustice. Whenever we do good, God works in us and with us to make us work.

(10) The help of God. Those who are reborn and have been healed should always implore the help of God, so that they may be able to attain the good end and persevere in good work.

(11) The making of vows. No one properly consecrates anything to God unless he promises something received from him, as we read, "And we give to you what we have received from your hand" [1 Chron. 29:14].

(12) How God loves us. God loves us as we will be by his own gift, not as we are by our merits.

(13) The restoration of free choice. The choice of the will which was weakened in the first human being can be restored only through the grace of baptism. Once something is lost, it can be returned only by someone who could give it in the first place. Thus Truth himself says, "If the Son sets you free, then you will be free indeed" [John 8:36].

(14) No one in trouble is freed from any kind of difficulty unless God's mercy intervenes for him. Thus the Psalmist says, "Your mercy goes quickly before us, Lord" [Ps. 79:8] and "My God will go before me with his mercy" [Ps. 59:10].

(15) Through his own iniquity, Adam was changed for the worse from what God had made him. Through God's grace the one who is faithful is also changed, but for the better, from what iniquity has done to him. That change was of the first transgressor; this one, according to the Psalmist, "is the change of the right hand of the Most High" [Ps. 77:10].

(16) No one should glory in what he seems to possess as though he had not received it, or as though he could receive it because the letter outwardly either appeared so that he could read or sounded so that he could hear. For as the Apostle says, "If justice comes through the law, then Christ died in vain" [Gal. 2:21] and "Ascending on high, he took captivity captive; he bestowed gifts on humans" [Eph. 4:8]. Whoever possesses anything has it from him. Anyone who denies he has it from him either does not really possess it or will be deprived of what he does have.

(17) Christian courage. Worldly desire makes the Gentiles brave, but the charity of God makes Christians courageous. This charity is poured into our hearts not through our own choice of will, but through the Holy Spirit who is given to us [Rom. 5:5].

(18) No merits precede grace. Rewards are due for good works if they are performed; grace, which is not owed, precedes so that they will be performed.

(19) No one is saved without God's mercy. Human nature,

even had it remained in the integrity in which it was created, could by no means have saved itself without the assistance of its creator. Thus, since without God's grace it could not retain the salvation it had received, without God's grace how will it be able to gain the salvation it has lost?

(20) A person can do nothing good without God. God does many good things in a person which the person himself does not do, but the person does no good things which God does not provide that the person do.

(21) Nature and grace. As the Apostle truly says to those who wanted to be justified in the law and thus abandon grace, "If justice is from the law, then Christ died in vain" [Gal. 2:21], so those who think the grace which the faith in Christ receives and praises is actually nature itself are rightly addressed: "If justice is through nature, then Christ died in vain." The law had already been given, and it did not justify. Nature as well had already been given, and it did not justify. Thus Christ did not die in vain, so that the law might be fulfilled through him who said, "I did not come to abolish the law but to fulfill it" [Matt. 5:17]. So too nature, which was ruined through Adam, was restored through him who said he had come to seek and to save what had perished [Luke 19:10].

(22) The things which are proper to humans. Of himself, no one has anything but lies and sin. If a person has any truth and justice, this comes from that spring for which we should thirst in this desert, so that by being moistened by a few drops from it we may not fail in the way.

(23) The divine and human wills. When people do what displeases God, they do their own will, not God's. When, however, they serve the divine will in doing what they will, although they perform their actions voluntarily, what they do is actually the will of him who prepares and commands what they will [Prov. 8:35].

(24) The vine and the branches. Branches are in a vine not by giving anything to the vine but by receiving their life from it. A vine is in its branches by supplying them with life-giving nourishment, not by receiving it from them. Thus for Christ

117

to remain in them and for them to remain in Christ are both profitable for his disciples, but not for Christ. If one branch is cut off, another can spring up from the living stock; but the branch which is cut off cannot live without the stock.

(25) The love by which we love God. To love God is certainly a gift of God. His own gift makes us love him; he loves before he is loved. We were loved even when we displeased him, so that we might be changed to please him. The Spirit of the Father and the Son, whom we love along with the Father and the Son, has poured forth charity into our hearts [Rom. 5:5].

THE DEFINITION OF FAITH

Thus according to the judgment of the Holy Scriptures and the decisions of the ancient fathers which have been written above, by the help of God we should both believe and proclaim that free choice had been so bent down and weakened through the sin of the first human being that afterward no one could love God as he should or believe in God or do what was good for God's sake unless the grace of the divine mercy intervened on his behalf. Thus we believe that the glorious faith which the Apostle Paul proclaims in praising them was bestowed on the just man Abel, on Noah, Abraham, Isaac, Jacob, and the whole multitude of ancient saints through the grace of God, not through the good of nature which had been given earlier in Adam. We both believe and know that even after the coming of the Lord all those who desire to be baptized do not hold this grace in free choice but receive it by the liberality of Christ. This has already been said so often· Paul preaches it thus: "For Christ's sake it is given to you not only to believe in him but also to suffer for him" [Phil. 1:29] and also "God who began this good work in you will complete it on the day of our Lord" [Phil. 1:6] and also "You were saved by grace through faith, and this is not from you but is God's gift" [Eph. 2:8]. When the Apostle says of himself, "I received mercy to be faithful" [1 Cor. 7:25], note that he did not say "because I was" but "to be faithful." Scripture also says, "What have you that you have not received" [1 Cor. 4:7] and "Every good and perfect gift descends from above from the Father of lights" [James 1:17] and "No one has anything unless it is given him from above" [John 3:27]. Innumerable passages of Holy Scripture could be brought forward to manifest this grace. For the sake of brevity they are omitted, since in fact a person who is not satisfied with a few will not be helped by more.

According to the Catholic faith, we also believe that once grace has been received through baptism, all the baptized, if they are willing to labor faithfully, with Christ's help and cooperation can and should fulfill what belongs to the soul's salvation. Not only do we not believe ourselves that the divine power predestines anyone to evil, but we also completely detest and condemn any who choose to believe such a terrible thing.

We also vigorously proclaim and believe that in every good work we do not first begin ourselves and subsequently receive help by God's mercy, but that without any preceding good merits he first inspires in us both faith and love of himself, so that we will faithfully seek the sacrament of baptism and then with his help be able to fulfill the things which please him after baptism. Obviously, then, all should believe that the wonderful faith of that thief whom the Lord called back to the homeland of paradise [Luke 23:39–43], of the centurion Cornelius to whom the Lord sent an angel [Acts 10:1–48], and of Zacchaeus, who merited to receive the Lord himself [Luke 19:1–10], was not from nature, but was given by the abundance of divine grace.

Moreover, because we desire and wish that our definition which is written above might be a remedy not only for religious persons but for the laity as well, we agreed that the distinguished and honorable men who have joined us to celebrate this festival would sign it with their own hands.

I, Caesarius, bishop in the name of Christ, have reread and

subscribed our declaration. I date it on the fifth day before the nones of July in the year of consulate of Decius the Younger [3 July 529].

[There follow the signatures of a dozen bishops.]

I, Peter Marcellinus Felix Liberius, the honorable and distinguished Praetorian Prefect of the Gauls and a nobleman, consent and subscribe.

[There follow half a dozen signatures of distinguished men.]

SELECTIONS FROM THE HOLY FATHERS

Some might say that an insistence on grace is new and novel, and that no one else advanced this issue as often and insistently as the holy Bishop Augustine. We thought, therefore, that we should append some passages from their writings in which one can see what Pope Innocent of the city of Rome preached when he occupied the Apostolic See, what the holy Bishop Ambrose of Milan thought, and what the holy Jerome declared. Thus a person who up to this point has believed without reflection and more naively than he should must not hesitate to guide and conform his mind to the standard of such fathers.

(1) The holy Augustine said: "The venerable Bishop Innocent gave this judgment to the Council of Carthage: 'Adam once bore freedom of choice; then he used this endowment inconsiderately. He fell into the depths of transgression and then found no way he could get out. He was eternally deceived by his freedom. The graciousness of Christ when he came later raised up the one who would otherwise have been buried under the burden of his downfall. Through the new purification of rebirth, he cleansed every past sin by the washing of his baptism.'

"Could anything be clearer or more straightforward than this judgment of the Apostolic See? Pelagius' disciple Caelestius proclaimed his agreement with it: 'I condemn everything according to the judgment of your predecessor Innocent.' " [Augustine, *Against Two Letters of the Pelagians*

II.iv.6; Innocent, *Letter 29*, 7 (which is *Letter 181* among Augustine's letters).]

(2) The holy Ambrose approves the statement that we have faith not from free choice but from the grace of God. He says in his Easter hymn: "Restoring faith to the ruined, / Lighting the face of the blind." ["This Is the True Day," ll. 5, 6.] The mercy of Christ restored the faith which the sin of Adam ruined.

(3) The same holy Augustine says: "The Pelagians claim that the human person initiates merit, which God then rewards with an increase of grace. The worthy Ambrose rejects even this assertion of theirs by saying, 'Since human effort is too weak to correct itself without divine assistance, it seeks God as a helper.'" [*Against Two Letters of the Pelagians* IV.xi.30.]

(4) Similarly, in his *On Flight from the World* Ambrose says: "We speak a great deal about flight from the world; would that our care and diligence in doing it matched the ease with which we discuss it. Even worse, however, is the way the attraction of worldly desires breaks in and a flood of useless concerns spreads over the mind, so that you end up turning over in your mind and thinking about precisely what you are attempting to escape. To guard against this is difficult for a human being; to avoid it completely is impossible. It remains something more hoped for than accomplished, as the prophet witnesses, 'Direct my heart to your testimonies and not to avarice' [Ps 119:36]. Our heart and our thoughts are not under our control. They confuse the mind and soul with the unexpected and draw you where you did not intend to go. They call you back the things of this world, implant secular concerns, intrude pleasures, and weave in enticements. Just as we prepare to lift up our minds, we get involved in frivolous thoughts and are usually cast down to earthly things. Who is so blessed that in his heart he always rises up? How could this happen without divine assistance? No way at all! The same book of Scripture says earlier, 'Blessed is the one whose help is from you, O Lord; you ar-

range the ascents of his heart' '' [Ps. 84:5]. [*On Flight from the World* I.1.]

What clearer or more adequate could be said? Still the Pelagians might reply that human merit precedes in the request for divine assistance, that this prayer makes a person worthy of being helped by divine grace. They should notice, then, what the same holy man says in his exposition of Isaiah, "Even to pray to God is a spiritual grace; 'no one proclaims Jesus Lord except in the Holy Spirit' '' [1 Cor. 12:3]. [*On Isaiah*, fragment 3.]

So too, in explaining Luke's Gospel, he says: "Certainly ʃou perceive that the Lord's power everywhere cooperates with human effort. Thus no one could build without the Lord or even begin without the Lord" [Ps. 127:1]. [*Exposition of the Gospel According to Luke* II.84.]

Does the holy Ambrose destroy free choice because he makes these statements and praises God's grace with grateful piety like a man of the promise? Or does he intend that grace which, for all their different circumlocutions, the Pelagians refuse to acknowledge as anything but the law, so that we should believe that God helps us not to do what we know but to know what we ought to do? If we suppose that this is what this man of God thinks, then we should hear what he says about the law itself. In his book *On Flight from the World* he says, "The law could shut everyone's mouth, but it could not convert the mind." Elsewhere in the same book he says, "The law condemns the deed but does not take away the iniquity." [*On Flight from the World* III.15; VII.39.]

They should notice that this faithful, Catholic man agrees with the Apostle who writes, "We know, however, that because whatever the law says, it says to those under the law, so that every mouth may be shut and the whole world may be subjected to God, because all flesh shall not be justified before him by the law" [Rom. 3:19–20]. The holy Ambrose derived his statement from this Apostolic expression.

(5) The holy Jerome says in exposition of Psalm 88: "A person caught in a storm takes cover under a rock or a roof. One

pursued by enemies flees to the walls of cities. A traveler worn out by sun and dust seeks respite in the shade. If a wild beast thirsts for someone's blood, the person does whatever he can to escape the danger. In the same way, the human person takes God for his helper from the beginning of his creation. Since he was created by his grace, and subsists and lives by his mercy, he can do no good work without him. God allowed him free choice in such a way that he would not deny his grace through his individual works. He was created free so that he would know that he would be nothing without God, and thus his freedom would not result in his own arrogance and in insult to his creator.

"When he says, 'Unto generation and generation' [Ps. 89:1], he means all times: before the law, under the law, under the gospel. Thus the Apostle says, 'You were saved by grace through faith; this is not from you but is God's gift' [Eph. 2:8]. In the salutations of all his letters, Paul does not mention peace until after he refers to grace. Grace comes first and peace follows, since the Lord who forgives our sins gives us his peace. Where does this leave people who congratulate themselves on the power of free choice, who think they have received God's grace because they have the capacity to either perform or not perform good or evil? Notice that here the blessed Moses asks that the splendor of the Lord his God may be upon those who have arisen, that he shine in the bodies and souls of the saints, that he direct the works of their hands and make them endure forever, that he confirm whatever good appears in the saints" [Ps. 90:17]. [*Letter 140,* 5, 21.]

(6) The same Jerome says the same thing in the book he entitled with the names of Atticus and Critobolus. (This title is given in the letter contained in its first book.)

"Again, then, what of the charge they advance that we destroy free choice? On the contrary, let them understand that freedom of choice is actually ruined by those who abuse it in doing evil, acting contrary to the generosity of its giver. Who then destroys choice? The person who thanks God, who credits the spring with whatever flows in his own stream? Or is it not rather the person who says to God, 'Depart from me, for I am pure [Isa. 65:5]. I do not consider you necessary. You gave me freedom of choice once and for all so that I could do what I want. Why do you interfere now, making me unable to accomplish anything unless you first complete your gifts in me?'

"Your discussion of God's grace is deceitful. In order to avoid the appearance of endangering free choice, you locate grace in the creation of human beings and do not look for it in individual actions. You belittle God's assistance and seek human support instead. I ask you to listen to this blasphemy: 'If I want to bend my finger, to move my hand, to sit, stand, walk, run, spit, or pick my nose with both my little fingers at once, do I need God's help to accomplish all this?' You ingrate, you blasphemer! Listen to the preaching of the Apostle: 'Whether you eat or drink or whatever else you do, do it all in the name of the Lord' [1 Cor. 10:31]. Listen to James: 'Notice what you are saying, "Today we will spend a year there doing business and making a profit." Are you sure of tomorrow? What is your life? It is a breeze, a mist which appears for a while and then blows away. You should say instead, "If the Lord wills and if we are alive, we will do this or that." As it is, you boast in your arrogance. This kind of self-glorification is very bad' [James 4:13–16].

"You think you are being insulted and freedom of choice is being destroyed if you constantly have recourse to God your Creator, if you depend upon his will and say, 'My eyes are always on the Lord because he freed my feet from the snare' [Ps. 25:15]. Will you dare to proclaim in bold tones, 'Everyone is governed by his own choice'? If each is governed by his choice, what room remains for God's help? If no one needs Christ as a guide, how can Jeremiah say, 'A person's path will not be in himself' [Jer. 10:23] and 'A person's steps are guided by the Lord' " [Prov. 20:24]. [*Letter 133*, 6–7.]

(7) Similarly, in the book *Atticus and Critobolus*, " 'Tell your sins that you may be justified [Isa. 43:26]. God shut up

everything under sin so that he could have mercy on all' [Rom. 11:32]. The highest justice a human being can attain is to consider any virtue he might have, not as his own but as the Lord's who gave it." [*Dialogue Against the Pelagians* I.13.]

(8) Again: " 'For behold all generations will call me blessed because he who is mighty has done great things for me and holy is his name. His mercy is from descendant to descendant on those who fear him. He has made power in his arm' [Luke 1:48–51]. Notice that in this she [Mary] calls herself blessed, not because of her own merit or virtue but because of the mercy of God dwelling in her." [*Dialogue Against the Pelagians* I.16.]

(9) Again, somewhat later: "What Christian could tolerate listening to what you say elsewhere, 'All are governed by their own will'? What room remains for God's help if not one, nor a few, nor many, but all are governed by their own will? How do you explain 'A person's steps are guided by the Lord' [Prov. 20:24]? or elsewhere, 'What have you that you have not received? If you have received it, why do you boast as though you had not?' [1 Cor. 4:7]. The Lord and Savior says, 'I did not come down from heaven to do my own will but the will of the Father who sent me' [John 6:38]. And elsewhere, 'Father, if it be possible, let this chalice pass from me; not, however, what I will but what you will' [Luke 22:42]. And in the Lord's Prayer, 'Your will be done on earth as it is in heaven' [Matt. 6:10]. Do you want to rule out all God's protection by your opinion, your rashness? In another place you lamely try to add, 'Not without God's grace.' Your meaning there can be grasped from what you say here, when you relate his grace not to individual actions but to the environment and laws, to the capacity for free choice. [*Dialogue Against the Pelagians* I.27.]

(10) There again, "When the human person was placed in honor, he did not understand it. He equated himself with the stupid cattle and became like them" [Ps. 49:20].

[*Dialogue Against the Pelagians* II.19.] The question here is whether a person who has become like the cattle can either plan or accomplish anything good without God's grace.

(11) The holy Jerome says again, " 'He saved them for nothing' [Ps. 56:7]. Doubtless, the just are saved by God's mercy rather than because of their own merit." [*Dialogue Against the Pelagians* II.19.]

(12) The point is that all the just, even those who lived before the coming of Christ, were saved by God's grace.

(13) "In order that we may realize that every good we do is from God, 'I will plant them so that they will never be uprooted, and I will give them perception and judgment so that they may know me' [Jer. 24:6–7]. If perception and judgment are given by God, if knowledge of the Lord springs from the root of the one we are to know, then where is the proud boasting of free choice?" [*Dialogue Against the Pelagians* II.27.]

(14) There again: "The prophet Daniel said to Nebuchadnezzar that the Most High rules over human sovereignty and gives it to whomever he wills. He establishes the lowly and downtrodden as a king, doing whatever he chooses [Dan. 4:17]. On this point, ask him what reason God has for establishing the lowly and despised. Further, pursue the question of the justice of his will, which is described, 'He lifts up the humble from the ground and from the dung heap he honors the poor, to set him with the rulers, with the princes of his people' " [Ps. 113:7–8]. [*Dialogue Against the Pelagians* II.30.]

(15) Again a bit later: "The Lord said to his disciples, 'I am the vine and you are the branches. Whoever remains in me and I in him bears much fruit because without me you can do nothing' [John 15:5]. As the shoots and branches of a vine wither as soon as they are cut from the stem, so too a person's whole strength fails and perishes if God's help abandons him. 'No one can come to me unless my Father has drawn him,' he says [John 6:44]. In saying 'No one can come to me,' he breaks the haughty freedom of choice. Unless what follows also happens, 'Unless my father draws him,' a person's desire

and effort to come to Christ are useless and unsuccessful. We might also remark here that one who is drawn does not run of his own accord; rather is he pulled along reluctant and sluggish or unwilling." [*Dialogue Against the Pelagians* III.9.]

(16) There again: "O man, you have been cleansed in the washing and you are described by 'Who is this that comes up all white, leaning on her cousin?' [Song of Sol. 8:5]. Indeed, she has been washed, but she cannot preserve her purity unless the Lord supports her" [*Dialogue Against the Pelagians* III.15].

If anyone thinks, as was said above, that only the holy Augustine insistently urged God's grace and in this sense believes that he disagreed with the holy Jerome, he should read the passage quoted below and see how Jerome praised the holy Augustine in this undertaking. Once he has read it, he should recognize that they spoke in one spirit and should cease to complain about God's grace.

(17) Section from the same book of the holy Jerome in praise of the holy Bishop Augustine. He says: "The holy and eloquent Bishop Augustine addressed two books on the baptism of infants to Marcellinus, who was later killed by heretics because of the envy of the tyrant Heraclianus, although he was innocent. In these books he opposes your heresy, the Pelagian one, in which you seek to explain the baptism of infants as given for the kingdom of heaven rather than the forgiveness of sins by using the text from the Gospel 'Unless a person is born again of water and the Spirit, he cannot enter the kingdom of heaven' [John 3:5]. He also wrote a third book for Marcellinus against those, that is, you people, who say that a person can be free of all sin if he wills it even without God's grace. More recently, he wrote a fourth book for Hilary opposing a teaching which invents many perverse things. I hear that some other books attack you by name, but I have not yet got my hands on them. I think, therefore, that I should lay this project aside. If I do not, someone will quote Horace to me: 'Do not carry wood into a forest' [*Satires* I.10.34]. We would either say the same things unnecessarily

or, if we tried to make new points, find that the better positions have already been staked out by that brilliant mind.'' [*Dialogue Against the Pelagians* III.19.]

Notice the praise with which the holy Jerome honored and extolled the blessed Augustine. Thus we believe that the judgments of fathers of such stature and position which we have quoted are adequate to recommend God's grace to the satisfaction of the minds of all.

Bibliography

PRIMARY SOURCES

Ambrose. *De Fuga Saeculi*, in *Corpus Scriptorum Ecclesiasticorum Latinorum*, vol. 32/ii, edited by C. Schenkl. Vienna, 1897. Pp. 163–207.

———. *Expositio Evangelii sec. Lucam*, in *Corpus Christianorum*, Series Latina, vol. 14, edited by M. Adriaen. Turnholt, 1957.

Augustine, *De Gratia Christi*, in *Corpus Scriptorum Ecclesiasticorum Latinorum*, vol. 42, edited by C. Urban and J. Zycha. Vienna, 1902. Pp. 125–66.

———. *De Correptione et Gratia*, in *Patrologia Latina*, vol. 44, edited by J.-P. Migne. Paris, 1865. Cols. 915–46.

de Clercq, C., ed. *Concilia Galliae (A.D. 511–695)*, in *Corpus Christianorum*, Series Latina, vol. 148A. Turnholt, 1963. Pp. 53–76.

Gregory of Nyssa. *De Beatitudinibus*, in *Patrologia Graeca*, vol. 44, edited by J.-P. Migne. Paris, 1863. Cols. 1193–302.

Irenaeus. *Irénée de Lyon, Contre les Hérésies IV*, in *Sources Chrétiennes*, vol. 100, edited by A. Rousseau. Paris, 1965.

Jerome. *Epistulae*, in *Corpus Scriptorum Ecclesiasticorum Latinorum*, vol. 56, edited by I. Hilberg. Vienna, 1918. Pp. 241–60 269–89.

Munier, C. ed *Concilia Africae (A.D. 345–525)*, in *Corpus Christianorum*, Series Latina, vol. 149. Turnholt, 1974.

Pelagius. *Ad Demetriadem*, in *Patrologia Latina*, vol. 30, edited by J. P. Migne. Paris, 1846. Cols. 15–46.

——— *Libellus Fidei ad Innocentium Papam*, in *Patrologia*

Latina, vol. 45, edited by J.-P. Migne. Paris, 1845. Cols 1716–18.

SECONDARY WORKS

Bouyer, L. *The Spirituality of the New Testament and the Fathers.* Vol. 1 of *History of Christian Spirituality.* Translated by Mary P. Ryan. New York: Desclée & Co., 1960.

Brown, P. *Augustine of Hippo: A Biography.* London: Faber & Faber, 1967; Berkeley: University of California Press, 1969.

————— . *Religion and Society in the Age of Augustine.* New York: Harper & Row, 1972; London: Faber & Faber, 1972.

Burnaby, J. *Amor Dei: A Study of the Religion of St. Augustine.* London: Hodder & Stoughton, 1938.

Burns, J. P. *The Development of Augustine's Doctrine of Operative Grace.* Paris: Études Augustiniennes, 1980.

————— . "The Economy of Salvation: Two Patristic Traditions," *Theological Studies* 37 (1976): 598–619.

Cherniss, H. F. *The Platonism of Gregory of Nyssa.* University of California Publications in Classical Philology, vol. 11. Berkeley: University of California Press, 1930.

Evans, R. *Pelagius: Inquiries and Reappraisals.* London: A. & C. Black, 1968; New York: Seabury Press, 1968.

Ferguson, J. *Pelagius.* Cambridge: At the University Press, 1956.

Grant, R. M. *Augustus to Constantine.* New York: Harper & Row, 1970; London: Collins, 1971.

Jonas, H. *The Gnostic Religion.* 2d ed. Boston: Beacon Press 1963.

Kelly, J. N. D. *Jerome: His Life, Writings, and Controversies.* London: Duckworth, 1975; New York: Harper & Row, 1975.

TeSelle, E. *Augustine the Theologian.* London: Burns & Oates, 1970; New York: Herder & Herder, 1970.